LEGENDARY LOCALS

OF

GALLUP

NEW MEXICO

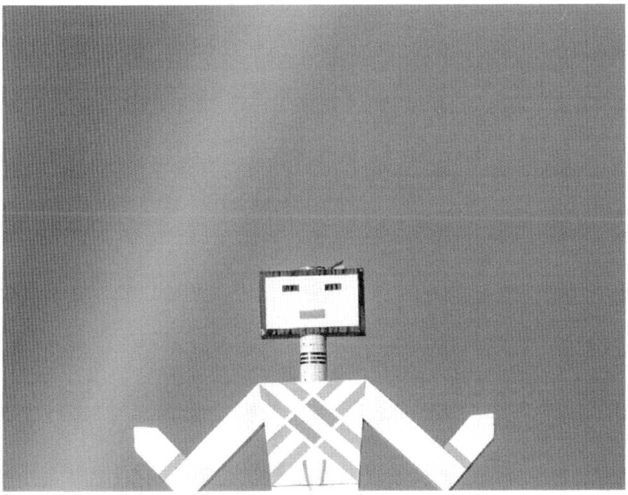

McKinley County Courthouse
The historic McKinley County Courthouse provides a picturesque backdrop for Gallup's popular Nightly Indian Dances each summer. According to Gallup Works Progress Administration (WPA) art researcher Carolyn Milligan, the courthouse, a New Deal architecture project, houses 19 oil paintings in addition to murals, tile work, lamps, and furniture created by New Deal artists and crafts workers. The signature piece in the courthouse is the Lloyd Moylan mural. (Courtesy of the *Gallup Independent*, Cable Hoover.)

Page 1: Summer Blessings in Gallup
Gallup's towering Navajo Yéí figure has greeted residents and visitors for decades. This image captures several blessings—the Yéí, a rainbow, and a summer rain shower. (Courtesy of the *Gallup Independent*, Adron Gardner.)

LEGENDARY LOCALS OF GALLUP NEW MEXICO

ELIZABETH HARDIN-BURROLA,
CAROL SARATH, AND BOB ROSEBROUGH

LEGENDARY LOCALS

Copyright © 2017 by Elizabeth Hardin-Burrola, Carol Sarath, and Bob Rosebrough
ISBN 978-1-4671-2567-3

Legendary Locals is an imprint of Arcadia Publishing
Charleston, South Carolina

Printed in the United States of America

Library of Congress Control Number: 2017942084

For all general information, please contact Arcadia Publishing:
Telephone 843-853-2070
Fax 843-853-0044
E-mail sales@arcadiapublishing.com
For customer service and orders:
Toll-Free 1-888-313-2665

Visit us on the Internet at www.arcadiapublishing.com

Dedication:
To those who work to make our community a better place for all.

On the Front Cover: Clockwise from top left:
Annie Wauneka, Navajo leader (courtesy of LBJ Presidential Library; see pages 17, 33), Hiroshi H. Miyamura, war hero (courtesy of the National Archives; see page 32), Mother Magda Garcia, faith leader (courtesy of the *Gallup Independent*; see page 90), Alex Seowtewa, artist (courtesy of the Seowtewa family; see page 110), Richard "Dick" Chavez, musician (courtesy of the *Gallup Independent*; see page 119), Zuni Olla Maidens, traditional dancers (courtesy of the *Gallup Independent*; see page 46), Joe Yurcic, athlete (courtesy of Josephine Yurcic; see page 64), Octavia Fellin, librarian (courtesy of Octavia Fellin Public Library; see page 67), Carl Gorman, artist (courtesy of C.N. Gorman Museum; see pages 109, 118).

On the Back Cover: From left to right:
Dwight D. Eisenhower, presidential candidate (courtesy of the City of Gallup, Ceremonial Collection, W.T. Mullarky; see page 47), Navajo delegation to Washington, DC, historical leaders (courtesy of the National Anthropological Archives, Smithsonian Institution; see page 15).

CONTENTS

ACKNOWLEDGMENTS

When we set out to write this book, we had the goal of profiling individuals from the Gallup region who have made important contributions to Gallup's culture and history. It was a seemingly simple goal, but we soon realized how challenging it would be. We quickly amassed far too many names for this slim volume. Therefore, we apologize for omitting the many worthy individuals from all walks of life who have made important contributions to our community. For every person we have profiled, there are several more individuals who could have easily been included. We also apologize for the brevity of these profiles—how can one sum up the contributions of a lifetime in a few short sentences?

We would like to thank everyone who shared their stories and photographs with us. The greatest highlight of working on this project has been talking with area residents, hearing their amazing stories, and viewing treasured photographs.

We would particularly like to thank *Gallup Independent* publisher Bob Zollinger for sharing the images of *Independent* photographers. Today, as in past years, the *Independent* has employed a number of award-winning photographers who shoot impressive images on a daily basis. Chuck Van Drunen and the *Gallup Journey* were also instrumental is assisting us with this project by generously providing a number of wonderful contemporary images. We would also like to thank the City of Gallup, the staff of the Octavia Fellin Public Library, the Gallup Historical Society, and Rehoboth Christian School, all of which graciously shared historical images from their archives. Individuals like Beverley Guadagnoli-Davis, Shan Guadagnoli, John Kozeliski, and Martin Link shared additional historical images.

A special thank-you goes out to Karla Rivera, the office manager at the Rosebrough & Fowles Law Firm, who assisted us in many ways—all with a calm demeanor and friendly smile.

Lastly, we would like to recognize all the individuals who tirelessly work at nonprofits in Gallup, improving all our lives. In appreciation, author royalties are being donated to three such organizations: Adventure Gallup, Big Brothers Big Sisters Mountain Region, and gallupARTS.

INTRODUCTION

I got a lot of cowboy songs there, Indian songs, carnival songs, vaudeville kind of stuff.

—Bob Dylan

What is it about Gallup, New Mexico, that would make a young Bob Dylan spin fanciful stories about growing up here? What is it about Gallup that would cause Mother Teresa, now St. Teresa of Calcutta, to send her Missionaries of Charity to feed and shelter our addicted, our homeless? What is it about Gallup that would inspire novelist Tony Hillerman to set his tales of murder and mystery in the communities that surround us?

If there is a simple answer, maybe it is found in Gallup's greatest asset—its people.

Like the crazy quilts our grandmothers used to sew, the Gallup region is a lively mix of cultures. Not only do we have New Mexico's tri-cultural heritage of Native American, Hispanic, and Anglo, but we also have large numbers of people of Italian, Slavic, Asian, Greek, Dutch, and Middle Eastern descent thrown into the mix.

We also have a rich history. Present-day Gallup is located between the historic 19th-century US Army posts of Fort Defiance, Arizona, and Fort Wingate, New Mexico. Countless human stories of conflict and peacemaking efforts unfolded in the Navajo territory surrounding the forts. Window Rock, the capital of the Navajo Nation, was founded just across the state line. To the south of Gallup, the people of Zuni Pueblo have lived there for thousands of years. With the arrival of Spanish explorers in 1539, the Zuni became the first Native people in the Gallup region to encounter Europeans and North Africans. More recent arrivals have brought Mormon pioneers to found the community of Ramah, Franciscan friars to build Catholic churches and missions across the region, and Christian Reformed missionaries of Dutch descent to establish the community of Rehoboth.

Since its earliest beginnings, Gallup has been a stop along one of the Southwest's major east-west travel routes via stagecoaches, transcontinental rail lines, and later, interstate highways. During the heyday of the marriage between the Atchison, Topeka & Santa Fe Railway and the Fred Harvey Company, trainloads of travelers, tourists, scholars, and researchers traveled to Gallup to stay in its elegant El Navajo Hotel and explore the Native American history and culture of the region. And with Route 66 slicing through the middle of town, Gallup became momentarily cool for perhaps the first and only time in its existence. Almost everyone—from Nat King Cole to the Rolling Stones—wanted to get their kicks on Route 66. Gallup's El Rancho Hotel was built on the city's east side and became not only a landmark along Route 66, but also the home away from home for dozens of Hollywood stars filming mostly cowboy and Indian movies in our scenic red rock country.

Nowadays, Gallup remains a destination for travelers. Located between the Navajo Nation, the Pueblo of Zuni, and Acoma and Laguna Pueblos, it is the perfect base for exploring those tribal communities. Visitors from around the world continue to include the Gallup Inter-Tribal Indian Ceremonial and the Red Rock Balloon Rally in their vacation plans, along with side trips to see Chaco Canyon, Window Rock, Canyon de Chelly, El Morro National Monument, the Painted Desert, and Petrified Forest. And with the recent growth of Gallup's outdoor adventure opportunities, more visitors are adding hiking and mountain biking to their list of activities.

But along with our rich mix of cultures and world-class sites, the Gallup region has its jumble of contradictions, contrasts, and paradoxes. We sent Native American servicemen into World War I before they had been granted US citizenship, and we sent more Native servicemen into World War II before they could vote. We live in an area filled with remarkable natural beauty, but we experienced one of the country's worst environmental disasters with the Church Rock uranium mill spill of July 1979. Our local communities are rich in culture, but often struggle with poverty and substance abuse. Some of the most talented Native American jewelers call Gallup home, yet the city still struggles to keep out imported fake jewelry that hurts Native artisans and the city's reputation. Gallup has traditionally had an influential liquor industry, but when more than 1,000 area residents marched to Santa Fe in 1989, they drew state attention to Gallup's alcohol problems and New Mexico leaders listened.

Gallup has been accused of many things, but it has never been accused of being boring. It is a quirky community, and many of the individuals profiled in this book have quirky stories about what brought them here. More than a few planned to stay just a short time and ended up staying a lifetime. But all of them have made important contributions to local history and culture. Each has had a role in the region's lively mix of cultures, and some of them have contributed to Gallup's contradictions, contrasts, and paradoxes.

Gallup Inter-Tribal Indian Ceremonial Parade

Crowds line Coal Avenue to watch the Gallup Inter-Tribal Indian Ceremonial Parade in this undated photograph. (Courtesy of Octavia Fellin Public Library.)

CHAPTER ONE

History Makers

Although Gallup was not founded until 1881, many important events in the nation's history have taken place in the region. Almost 80 years before the Pilgrims landed in North America on the *Mayflower*, Spanish explorers were here, searching for the fabled Seven Golden Cities of Cibola. The disastrous arrival of Esteban the Moor into the Pueblo of Zuni in 1539, and his subsequent murder, marked the beginning of the Spanish presence in the region. The centuries that followed were characterized by conflict among and between people from widely diverse cultures—Apaches, Navajos, Pueblo people, Spanish, Mexicans, and Americans. For much of the time, it was a volatile mix.

In the two decades before Gallup's founding, both the country and the region were experiencing tumultuous times. Just as the United States was struggling to survive in the midst of the Civil War, the US Army and the Navajo people were locked in a bitter struggle that would result in the Diné people's Long Walk and incarceration at Hwéeldi, or Bosque Redondo. After the Navajos' return to their homeland, the ensuing dozen years led to westward expansion and an economic boom in the region.

As the headquarters for railroad construction in the 1880s, Gallup became an epicenter of frenetic energy as rail lines were laid, coal was mined, and lumber was harvested. Underground coal mining and railroading were dangerous jobs. Explosions, fires, horrific accidents, and derailments were an ever-present part of life. Coal strikes, initiated by union organizers, extended mining dangers beyond the underground shafts to the streets of Gallup as miners and management regularly clashed over wages and working conditions.

World War II brought more struggle as almost every family across the region sent their sons into harm's way in either the European or Pacific theater. And although the lives of about 100 local men hung in the balance in the aftermath of the Battle of Bataan in the Philippines, the local community rallied to support the many Japanese American families who had made Gallup their home.

Mirroring the rest of the country, Gallup struggled to deal with the political activism of the 1960s and 1970s. In particular, Native American activists raised issues about discrimination, exploitation, and the ever-present alcohol industry. Today, community leaders continue to grapple with the region's high levels of poverty, unemployment, and substance abuse.

But regardless of the challenges of each era, Gallup has always attracted strong-willed men and women who have produced a history that is raw, real, and compelling.

Esteban the Moor (c. 1500–1539)

From his birth in North Africa to his death in the Pueblo of Zuni, Esteban's brief life was packed with adventure, danger, and intrigue. Born in Morocco and enslaved by the Portuguese, Esteban's fate as a New World explorer was sealed when he was sold to a Spanish explorer who joined the ill-fated Narváez expedition to Florida in 1527. After Esteban and three other survivors made a harrowing eight-year journey to Mexico City, Esteban was pressed into service as the guide for Fray Marcos de Niza's 1539 search for the fabled Seven Cities of Cibola. Esteban's luck ran out in Zuni, where he was killed after reportedly making demands on the Zuni people. Esteban is portrayed by WPA artist Lloyd Moylan in this McKinley County Courthouse mural. (Courtesy of the *Gallup Independent*, Adron Gardner.)

Manuel Antonio Chaves (1818–1889)
Manuel Antonio Chaves, known as "el Leoncito," or "the Little Lion," was born during the end of the Spanish colonial period, spent his early adulthood under Mexican rule, and then lived the last decades of his life as a citizen of the US Territory of New Mexico. According to his biographer Marc Simmons, Chaves's life "was interwoven with almost every major historical event which occurred during his adult life—the Texan-Santa Fe Expedition, the Mexican War, the Civil War, skirmishes with Utes, Navajos, and Apaches." From age 16, when Chaves was the sole survivor of an attack on a slave raiding party in Navajo territory, to 1861, when he was commander of Fort Fauntleroy, later Fort Wingate, Chaves's life was representative of the conflict-filled 19th-century American West. (Courtesy of Charles Lummis Photographs, Special Collections, Claremont Colleges Library, Claremont, California.)

James Henry Carleton (1814–1873)

Gen. James Henry Carleton had the attributes that made heroes of many men in the 19th century American West. Carleton was a man of driving ambition with an unrelenting work ethic. He was also a Christian idealist and perfectionist, incapable of admitting a mistake or changing his mind. As military commander of New Mexico, Carleton was convinced that the solution to conflicts with Navajos was to move the entire tribe to Bosque Redondo where he believed the Diné people would, for their own good, become Christian farmers. After four years of illness, floods, hail storms, and crop failures, Carleton's social experiment was recognized as a failure, and the surviving Navajos were permitted to return home. Brevet Brigadier General Carleton was photographed in Santa Fe around 1866. (Courtesy of the Palace of the Governors Photo Archives, NMHM/DCA, No. 022938.)

Kit Carson (1809–1868)

After leading volunteers in New Mexico's encounter with the Civil War and then subduing the Mescalero Apaches, General Carleton ordered Kit Carson to Fort Wingate to prepare for war against the Navajos. Carson, who had joined the US Army to fight Confederates, not Native Americans, resigned. For reasons unknown to history, Carson relented, and in the summer of 1863, he headed west with 1,000 men toward the canyons, mesas, and mountains of the rugged Diné homeland. By leading a scorched earth battle of attrition that culminated during the winter in early 1864 in Canyon de Chelly, Carson forced starving Navajos to begin surrendering in waves. The paradoxical life of Kit Carson, who had married two Native American women, is explored in the acclaimed *Blood and Thunder* by Hampton Sides. (Courtesy of the Palace of the Governors Photo Archives, NMHM/DCA, No. 007151.)

Manuelito (c. 1818–1893) and Pedro Pino (c. 1788–1880s)

Two of the most influential 19th-century Native leaders in the local region were Manuelito, of the Navajo tribe, and Pedro Pino, of the Pueblo of Zuni. Their lives spanned much of the century leading up to the founding of Gallup. Their life experiences reflected the tumultuous history of the period, the conflicts between culture groups, and the challenges faced by Native people in their dealings with representatives of Spain, Mexico, and eventually, the United States. According to historians, Manuelito (above left) was born in the Bears Ears region of southeastern Utah. But as an adult, he had married a daughter of the Navajo leader Narbona and was living in the region north of present-day Gallup. Manuelito gained a reputation as a tenacious warrior who defiantly resisted Mexican and American incursions into Diné territory. This resistance continued throughout the US Army's campaign to subjugate the Navajo people and force them on the Long Walk to the desolate Hwéeldi, or Bosque Redondo. Manuelito finally surrendered in 1866, but once at Bosque Redondo, he continued to advocate for his people's return to Dinétah, their traditional homeland. With the signing of the Treaty of 1868 and the Navajo people's return home, Manuelito continued to be a revered Diné leader who promoted the importance of education. About 30 years before Manuelito's birth, a Pueblo man named Lai-iu-ah-tsai-lu was born to the A:shiwi, or Zuni people. He would eventually become known by his Spanish name, Pedro Pino, and become one of the most important governors of Zuni Pueblo. According to E. Richard Hart, Pino's biographer, Lai-iu-ah-tsai-lu was about 14 when he was captured by a group of Navajos while traveling with a Zuni war party. He then lived among the Diné people for about two years and learned the Navajo language. Before long, however, he was sold into slavery in a Spanish household in New Mexico, possibly the household of Don Pedro Bautista Pino, a wealthy, influential, and politically connected colonist living in Santa Fe. During this time, Lai-iu-ah-tsai-lu assumed the name Pedro Pino, became fluent in Spanish, and gained an understanding of the workings of the Spanish colonial government. Eventually, Pino returned to Zuni and rose to prominence as a tribal leader for much of the remainder of the century. He is pictured above right, seated at center in an 1879 photograph of six Zuni men taken by John K. Hillers. (Left, courtesy of the Library of Congress, digital file No. LC-USZ62-98365; right, courtesy of the National Archives, identifier No. 523634.)

Jesus Arviso (c. 1847–1932)

When Jesus Arviso was born in Sonora, Mexico, in the mid-1800s, no one could have predicted the role he would play in Navajo history. As a young child, Arviso was kidnapped by Apaches, and later traded to a Navajo in exchange for a horse. Living among the Navajo people, Arviso became fluent in the language, which led to his roles as an interpreter—from Navajo to Spanish—and as a guide for US troops. Arviso first served as an intermediary in 1860, when he was sent by a band of Navajos, carrying a white sheepskin to wave, to ask for a truce with American forces. Arviso went on to serve as a military guide and an interpreter at Fort Wingate and later Fort Sumner. After the Long Walk, Arviso married his first wife, a Navajo woman named Yohazbaa', while Navajos were being held at the despised Bosque Redondo. Arviso was later an interpreter for the Treaty of 1868, which allowed the Navajo people to return to their beloved Dinétah. Arviso returned to the Navajo homeland as well, continued to act as an intermediary between the Navajo and the federal government, and took a second Navajo wife. In 1874, Arviso accompanied a Navajo delegation to Washington, DC. When Dr. Washington Matthews, the noted surgeon, ethnologist, and linguist, was stationed at Fort Wingate, Arviso and Chee Dodge helped Matthews record Navajo ceremonies and legends. In his later years, Arviso moved to Cubero, New Mexico, where he married a third wife, a Hispanic woman. Today, large numbers of Navajo people are descendants of Arviso and his first two wives. According to Gallup writer John Cabrera, his grandfather, Gallup police captain John B. Arvizo, was a grandson of Arviso and his third wife. John B. Arvizo was killed in the line of duty in September 1965, and the Gallup Department of Public Safety Building was rededicated in his memory. In this photograph by C.M. Bell, Jesus Arviso, standing at far right, is pictured with the Navajo delegation to Washington, DC, in 1874. Pictured are, from left to right, (seated) Carnero Mucho, Mariano, Juanita (Manuelito's wife), Manuelito, Manuelito Segundo (Juanita and Manuelito's son), and Tiene-su-se; (standing) "Wild Hank" Sharp, Ganado Mucho, Barbas Gueras, Indian Agent William Amy, "Rocky Mountain Bill" Taylor, Cabra Negra, Cayetanito, Narbona Primero, and Jesus Arviso. (Courtesy of the National Anthropological Archives, Smithsonian Institution, negative No. 2410-C.)

Dan DuBois (1835–1925)

Dan DuBois was a larger-than-life personality who associated with the famous and infamous of the Southwest. Called "Iron Shirt" by Navajos because of numerous wounds he survived, DuBois reportedly lived among the Apaches and Utes before settling in the Gallup area. During his 90 years, DuBois was a jack-of-all-trades who worked as a dispatch rider delivering mail, merchant seaman, Union soldier, stagecoach driver, rancher, interpreter, civilian scout, guide and camp manager for archaeologists, and a local Indian trader. Many area residents trace their ancestry back to DuBois and his Navajo wife Rosa, a daughter of Navajo leader Manuelito, or to DuBois and his Hispanic wife Doratea Escorcia. Pictured at the 1923 dedication of Gallup's El Navajo Hotel, DuBois talks with Navajo medicine man Hash-kay Yashi. (Courtesy of the University of Arizona Library Special Collections, Fred Harvey Collection.)

Henry Chee Dodge (1857–1947)

The identity of his father and the exact date of his birth are uncertain, but what is known is that Henry Chee Dodge was orphaned as a young boy when his father died and his mother disappeared searching for food. Dodge was adopted by strangers who found him abandoned and hungry on the side of a trail, and he was taken on the Navajo Long Walk in 1864 and marched 300 miles to Bosque Redondo. There was no doubt that Red Boy, or Kiiłchíí' as he was known, was a survivor and a quick learner. Upon his return to Dinétah, the Navajo homeland, Dodge was reunited with relatives while remaining with his adoptive family. He learned English and Spanish and worked as the official translator for the US Army in Fort Defiance, Arizona. He was also appointed chief of the Navajo Police and appointed chief of the Navajos in 1884 by the commissioner of Indian affairs while still in his twenties. During this time, Dodge became a successful stockman, farmer, and storekeeper while working on behalf of the Diné people. When the Navajo Tribal Council was formed in 1923, Dodge was elected the first chairman. There was some resistance to his election because he was not full-blooded Navajo, but he had become a well-respected spokesman and advocate for the Diné people, and he successfully held the position until 1928. Dodge would be reelected tribal chairman in 1942 when he was in his eighties. In 1946, he was elected to the position of vice-chairman, but he died of pneumonia before he could assume office. Having more than one wife was an accepted practice during the 1800s, and Dodge had multiple wives during his lifetime. He was also the father of six children. His son Tom also became tribal chairman, and his daughter Annie Dodge Wauneka was a tribal council member and a Presidential Medal of Freedom Award recipient. Dodge, who served on the board of Gallup's First State Bank, built a home in Gallup for one of his children that sits on a hill looking eastward to Church Rock and Pyramid Peak. In honor of Dodge's lifelong advocacy for the importance of education, the Gallup-McKinley County Schools built an elementary school named in his honor in 1989. (Photograph by Ben Wittick, courtesy of the Palace of the Governors Photo Archives, NMHM/DCA, No. 015950.)

Fort Wingate's Buffalo Soldiers (late 1800s)

Nearly a dozen African American soldiers of the 9th Cavalry, one of the famed Buffalo Soldiers regiments, became recipients of the Congressional Medal of Honor during the US Indian Wars of the late 1800s. However, one officer refused a lieutenant colonelcy commanding Buffalo Soldiers. That officer—George Armstrong Custer—later went on to infamy and death at the Battle of the Little Big Horn in 1876. In New Mexico, Buffalo Soldiers saw most of their military action in campaigns against the Apaches. Locally, Buffalo Soldiers were assigned to Fort Wingate after the Diné people returned from Bosque Redondo to their homeland in 1868. Noncommissioned officers from Troop L, 9th Cavalry are shown at Fort Wingate in this 1899 photograph. (Courtesy of the Palace of the Governors Photo Archives, NMHM/DCA, No. 098373.)

David L. Gallup (1842–1924) Mystic, Connecticut, native David L. Gallup did not live here long, but it was long enough to leave his name on the town. Gallup, a railroad paymaster, came here in 1880 when the former stagecoach stop became the construction headquarters for the westward expansion of the railroad. On paydays, railroad employees would "go to Gallup," so the name stuck. According to Gallup family historians, Gallup moved back east where he worked as controller for the Santa Fe Railway and was a well-known figure in the New York railroad financial and banking district. Gallup was related to other famous members of the Gallup family tree, including poet Emily Dickinson, Pres. George H.W. Bush, Pres. George W. Bush, and George H. Gallup, the founder of the famous Gallup Poll. (Right, courtesy of the City of Gallup; below, courtesy of the Octavia Fellin Public Library.)

St. Katharine Drexel (1858–1955)
When wealthy Philadelphia heiress Katharine Drexel decided to become a Catholic sister and establish a religious order dedicated to serving African American and Native American people, the *Philadelphia Public Ledger* ran a banner headline: "Miss Drexel Enters a Catholic Convent—Gives Up Seven Million." That decision—by one of the most remarkable women in American history—has had a positive and lasting impact in the Gallup area. Drexel turned down a life of wealth and privilege to take up a life of poverty and prayer, hardship and service. Drexel's religious order, the Sisters of the Blessed Sacrament, built churches and schools in African American and Native American communities, promoted racial integration and equality in the Catholic Church and American society, and faced down bigoted laws and opponents. Although well educated, widely traveled, and prominent in Philadelphia society, Drexel began contemplating religious life while caring for her step-mother, Emma Bouvier, who died of cancer in 1883. (First Lady Jacqueline Bouvier Kennedy Onassis was a descendant of the Bouvier family.) Drexel reportedly was influenced by the fact that her family's wealth could not save Emma's life. After her father's death in 1885, Drexel and her sisters became heiresses to his $15.5 million estate, and they began to follow their devout parents' example of sharing their wealth with charitable causes. Drexel and her sisters supported missions on Indian reservations and met with Oglala Lakota leader Chief Red Cloud. They also traveled to Rome and had a private audience with Pope Leo XIII. When Drexel entreated the pope to send missionaries to Native Americans, the pope challenged Drexel to become a missionary herself. Within a few years, she did just that. Locally, Drexel purchased land in what is now St. Michaels, Arizona, recruited Franciscan friars to begin ministry on the Navajo Reservation, and founded St. Michael Indian School. In the 1900s, a number of Gallup area Native American women joined Drexel's religious order. Drexel was canonized a Roman Catholic saint in October 2000. Pope John Paul II celebrated the Mass in Rome with a silver chalice handcrafted by local Zuni artist Carlton Jamon. Drexel, far right, is shown holding the hand of Adzan Yazzie in this photograph taken in front of a trading post in Lukachukai, Arizona, about 1920. She is accompanied by Mother M. Francis Xavier McCann. (Both, courtesy of the Archives of the Sisters of the Blessed Sacrament.)

Early Rehoboth Founders

With the founding of the Rehoboth Mission in 1903, another ingredient was added to Gallup's melting pot of cultures. Mission workers with the Christian Reformed Church (CRC), mostly Dutch Americans and Dutch immigrants, first came to the region in the 1890s. According to Rehoboth historian Henry P. Ippel, the Rev. Herman Fryling and his wife, Kate, along with and Andrew and Effie VanderWagen, arrived with plans to establish a mission in Fort Defiance, Arizona, in 1896. That effort and a subsequent one stalled, but in 1902, the CRC denomination acquired the Smith Ranch, located just six miles east of Gallup. A year later, the Rehoboth Mission School opened as a boarding school for Native American students. The first six students, four boys and two girls, were recruited from Navajo families south of Gallup. As was typical of that boarding school era, the children's Navajo names were discarded and replaced with Anglo names. In this case, the students were renamed after prominent Christian missionaries. Rehoboth went on to establish a day school for local Anglo and Hispanic students in 1929, a public school for those students in 1938, and high school classes in 1940. In 1973, the mission school became Rehoboth Christian School. Along with its educational emphasis, Rehoboth also established the Rehoboth Mission Hospital in 1910. Under the leadership of Dr. Richard Pousma from 1927 to 1941, the Rehoboth Hospital's medical outreach and reputation grew. Pousma encouraged the admittance of non-Indian "pay patients" to bring in needed financial revenue, broaden the medical expertise of the staff, and promote goodwill in the Gallup community. According to Ippel, those pay patients increased from 14 in 1928 to 189 in 1940. Church officials, however, believed the hospital's primary mission was to treat Native American patients. The mission hospital went on to become Rehoboth Christian Hospital in 1964, and it later merged with McKinley General in 1983. Rehoboth High School was named one of the top 50 Christian high schools in the United States in 2014. This c. 1903 photograph shows the first six Rehoboth Mission students, from left to right, Henry Whipple, Clarissa Pierson, Gertrude Alger, Albert Gardiner, James Evans, and John Eliot. Behind them, early Rehoboth Mission founders, from left to right, Andrew VanderWagen, Nellie Noordhoff, Rev. Herman Fryling, and Rev. L.P. Brink pose with the students. (Courtesy of Rehoboth Christian School.)

Father Anselm Weber (1862–1921)

In 1898, when Mother Katharine Drexel purchased 160 acres west of Window Rock to establish St. Michael Indian School, she persuaded a province of mostly German American Franciscan friars from Cincinnati, Ohio, to begin a mission among the Diné people. As a result, in October 1898, Father Anselm Weber arrived in Gallup by train, accompanied by Father Juvenal Schnorbus and Brother Placid Buerger. Weber's life here would alter the course of local history. One of his first projects was to compile a Navajo dictionary. Weber and Schnorbus began working on the project with Charley and Sammy Day, sons of an Indian trader who were fluent in Navajo. Schnorbus and Charley started with the letter "A," and Weber and Sammy began at "Z." They met at the letter "I" on April 26, 1899. When Drexel was preparing to open the doors of St. Michael Indian School, Weber promoted the school through personal visits to traditional tribal headmen and Navajo families. He also assisted Diné headmen in organizing the tribe's system of self-government. The unusual term for Navajo local units of government—"chapters" —was borrowed from a Franciscan term the friars use for their religious order meetings. Weber was also frequently called upon to act as a mediator between Diné people and government officials, most notably during the Beautiful Mountain Uprising of 1913. That dispute centered on the polygamy of Hatahlie Yazhie and his three wives. Government officials escalated a confrontation with Yazhie and his band of supporters to the point that US troops were brought into Gallup for possible military action. Clearer heads prevailed, however, allowing Weber and Navajo interpreters to defuse the situation. The Catholic friar also advocated for Yazhie's group at trial, which resulted in brief jail sentences in Gallup. Weber, who was also trained as a surveyor, is probably best remembered for persistently advocating for Navajo land rights. According to Franciscan historians, Weber made repeated trips to Washington, DC, and wrote more than 3,000 letters to government and railroad officials advocating for the expansion of the Navajo Reservation. Franciscans credit Weber's efforts with adding 1,439,160 acres of land east and south of the reservation to Navajo holdings. A stained-glass window in Gallup's Sacred Heart Cathedral commemorates Weber's life. (Courtesy of the Archives of the Franciscan Province of Our Lady of Guadalupe of Albuquerque.)

Amasa Bemis McGaffey (1870–1929)

Vermont native A.B. McGaffey became a wealthy timber magnate in New Mexico after his move to Albuquerque in 1891. As a contractor supplying ties for the railroad's western expansion, McGaffey founded the lumber camp in the Zuni Mountains that grew into a small town named after him. Many local families—Anglo, Hispanic, and Navajo—are descendants of McGaffey lumbermen. On September 3, 1929, McGaffey boarded his first airplane flight, a Transcontinental Air Transport flight in Albuquerque. Near Mount Taylor, McGaffey's plane was struck by lightning and crashed, killing all aboard. The lumber town declined following McGaffey's death and the Great Depression. (Left, courtesy of Cobb Memorial Photography Collection, PICT 000-119-0193, Center for Southwest Research, University Libraries, University of New Mexico; below, courtesy of Gallup Historical Society.)

Arthur T. Hannett (1884–1966)

Arthur T. Hannett, author of the memoir *Sagebrush Lawyer*, arrived in Gallup May 1, 1911, after a traveling salesman told him there was a great opportunity for a lawyer in Gallup. During his first weeks in town, Hannett went to Kitchen's Opera House to see a prize fight on the second floor. After the fight, he went downstairs for a drink that was interrupted when a "short foreigner" with a sawed-off shotgun blew off the head of a man standing near Hannett. The man collapsed like an empty sack, causing Hannett to vomit. Seven years later, after making a name for himself as a trial lawyer battling coal companies, Hannett was elected mayor. In 1924, he was elected governor. One of Hannett's biggest accomplishments as governor was to establish the present alignment of Route 66. (Courtesy of the Library of Congress, No. LC-DIG-ggbain-30359.)

The Chihuahuita Coal Miner Evictions
In the spring of 1934, a land deal went down between Clarence Vogel and the Gallup American Coal Company. Vogel was a state senator and a political ally of the coal companies. The coal company sold Vogel a large tract of land that included the Chihuahuita neighborhood where many Mexican coal miners had built homes on coal company land. Vogel raised prices and then filed eviction suits against 75 coal miners seeking possession of the land on which they had built homes. In his role as state senator, Vogel successfully worked to defeat an anti-eviction bill that the coal miners' union introduced in the New Mexico legislature. Victor Campos was the first Chihuahuita coal miner to have an eviction notice nailed on his door in 1935. Campos was unemployed and could not read or write English. On April 1, 1935, sheriff's deputies, who were selected and paid by coal companies and who worked primarily as mine guards, moved a bed, armchair, and coal stove from Campos's home and placed them outside in the dirt. Campos and a couple of union members waited until dark and tore down boards that had been nailed to his front door and moved his belongings back into his home. Within an hour, Campos and his friends were arrested and taken to jail on charges of breaking and entering. The April 4, 1935, coal riot broke out moments after the conclusion of Campos's bond hearing. The events from this tumultuous time in Gallup's history became the inspiration for *The Gallup 14*, a novel written by former Gallup resident Gary L. Stuart, now an Arizona trial lawyer who teaches law and writing at Arizona State University. Stuart grew up just yards from the alley where the coal miners' riot took place. (Courtesy of Chuck Van Drunen.)

Mack R. Carmichael (1897–1935)
On April 4, 1935, during the bond hearing for Victor Campos and Exiquio Navarro, a vocal member of the coal miners' union, a crowd of miners gathered in front of the old courthouse. The crowd grew to over 100 and got progressively louder and more agitated. After Campos was put in a courthouse holding pen, Sheriff Mack Carmichael, along with his undersheriff and two deputies, took Navarro back to jail through the alley between Coal and Aztec. The crowd ran to Third Street and then pressed forward toward the lawmen and Navarro. Minutes later, after 15 shots were fired, the sheriff lay dead from a head wound, two miners were dead, one deputy was seriously wounded, and another one beaten. The prisoner Navarro escaped. Here, troops occupy Gallup during a miners' strike in the early 1900s in an undated photograph. (Courtesy of Gallup Historical Society.)

David Levinson (1885–1964)

When Philadelphia activist attorney David Levinson died in 1964, the *New York Times* described him as a "fighter for the underdog, frequently at his own expense and with no prospects of getting paid for his services." The newspaper quoted Levinson as saying, "As a Jew, I know what it means to suffer injustice, indignity and intolerance. My people have been lynched too." As a result, the newspaper said Levinson "repeatedly plunged into unpopular causes and more than once emerged from the fight with a bloody nose or a bruised head." This proved true for Levinson's stint in Gallup, after he came here to defend a group of coal miners accused of shooting Sheriff Mack Carmichael amid labor union strife with the Gallup-American Coal Company. According to union accounts, on May 2, 1935, Levinson, along with Robert Minor, a labor leader, journalist, and member of the American Communist Party, was meeting with Julia Bartol inside her car, which was parked in front of Gallup's El Navajo Hotel. Bartol was the wife of Joe Bartol, president of the Gallup local of the United Mine Workers of America and one of the jailed miners. The three were reportedly attacked by black-hooded gunmen in three cars, who kidnapped Levinson and Minor and threatened Bartol. Levinson and Minor were found the next day—miles away from Gallup—by a Navajo man who took them to a hospital in Tohatchi. Levinson and Minor claimed the vigilantes tied sacks on their heads, beat them, and threatened to kill them before dumping them in the desert. Although newspapers reported that Sheriff D.W. Roberts thought the kidnapping story was a hoax and District Attorney C.R. McIntosh's hospital conference with the men "broke up with shouts of 'liar' and 'frame-up,' " the incident made national news, and Gov. Clyde Tingley provided Levinson and Minor with police protection. According to one newspaper account, "They worked with pistols in their laps, the four state troopers provided by Governor Tingley at their backs." In this 1935 news photograph, Levinson is shown with a bandage on his head, accompanied by law enforcement officers. (Courtesy of the E. Hardin-Burrola collection.)

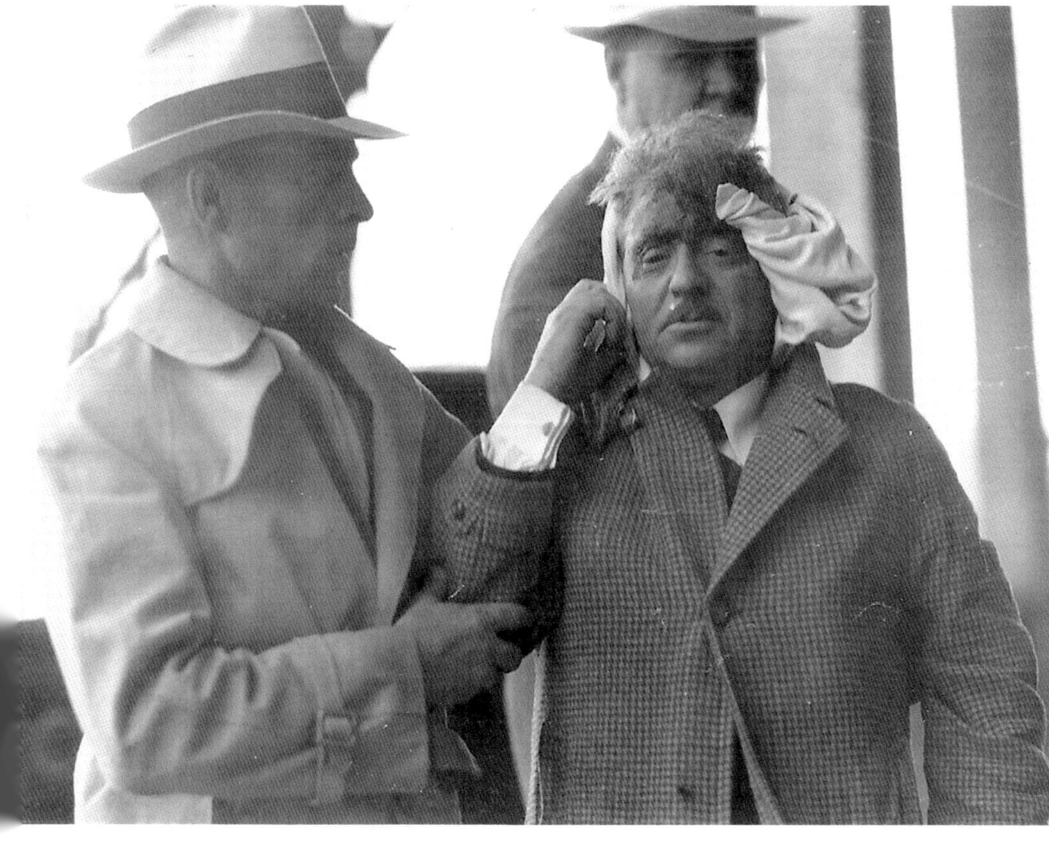

L.E. "Bobcat" Wilson (1907–1993)

Immediately before the 1935 coal miners' riot broke out in the alley behind the courthouse on Coal Street, Deputy L.E. "Bobcat" Wilson and Deputy Hoy Boggess were following Sheriff Mack Carmichael and Undersheriff Dee Roberts, who were on either side of the un-handcuffed prisoner, Exiquio Navarro, each holding one of Navarro's arms. The crowd, which circled into the alley from Third Street, pressed forward. Navarro began jostling with Carmichael and Roberts, trying to break free. Boggess threw an ill-advised tear gas canister that landed in the middle of the crowd, causing half of the crowd to press forward toward the lawmen rather than retreat. In the aftermath of the riot, Sheriff Carmichael and two of the miners were dead. Wilson had two bullet wounds, and Boggess had been beaten. Six men and one woman in the crowd were wounded. Boggess's gun was missing, and Navarro was gone. Gallup turned into an armed camp. 55 men were arrested within two hours, and over 100 people were placed in protective custody. Ultimately, 10 miners stood trial in Aztec, New Mexico, facing first-degree murder charges in Carmichael's death. The eyewitness testimony of Undersheriff Roberts and Deputies Wilson and Boggess was expected to be crucial to the prosecution's case. After the testimony of Roberts and Boggess, there were still many unanswered questions that courtroom observers expected Wilson's testimony to resolve. Neither Roberts nor Boggess had identified any of the defendants as the person who shot Carmichael. Inexplicably, the prosecution rested its case without calling Wilson as a witness. After only two and a half hours of deliberation, the jury returned a verdict finding all 10 defendants not guilty of first-degree murder. Three defendants were found guilty of second-degree murder, and the remaining seven defendants were found not guilty of all charges. The jury also made a request of clemency for the three convicted defendants. On appeal, the New Mexico Supreme Court overturned one of the three convictions, and four years after the trial, Governor Miles granted conditional pardons to the remaining two defendants. Given these factors, questions remain as to who shot and killed Sheriff Carmichael. Wilson went on to serve as sheriff himself for many years and to establish and operate the Rock Springs Ranch northwest of Gallup. (Courtesy of the *Gallup Independent*.)

World War II Servicemen

As in almost every community across the United States, virtually all Gallup families were affected by the sacrifices of World War II. For a small community, however, Gallup may have paid a higher price than most. Here are just three Gallup stories.

John Spinelli (1923–2001) was a ship's cook on the USS *Indianapolis* on July 30, 1945, when the ship was hit by two Japanese torpedoes. Within minutes, the *Indianapolis* began sinking. Of the 1,196 aboard, about 300 men died during the sinking, and about 900 men made it into the water. However, few life rafts were released, and rescuers did not arrive for nearly five days. After being subjected to shark attacks, hunger, thirst, exposure, and injury, only 317 men were pulled out alive. Spinelli survived the horrific ordeal and returned to Gallup.

Walter Shibata (1915–2001), a member of one of Gallup's pioneering Japanese American families, was a member of the famed US Army 442 Regimental Combat Team, reportedly the most decorated outfit in American military history. The 442nd was a segregated unit, consisting almost entirely of second-generation Japanese American citizens, including six local men. Shibata was taken prisoner by German soldiers on June 26, 1944, near Suvereto, Italy, liberated a year later on May 3, 1945, and then returned to Gallup.

On December 8, 1941, a day after the attack on Pearl Harbor, Japanese bombers attacked the Philippines, which led to the Battle of Bataan. The 200th Coast Artillery of the New Mexico National Guard—filled with dozens of Gallup men—is credited for first firing on the enemy. According to historian Eva Jane Matson, more than 100 men from McKinley County and surrounding reservation communities were serving in the Philippines. For four long months, 75,000 US and Filipino troops held off the Japanese until they were forced to surrender on April 9, 1942. As prisoners of war, the Americans and Filipinos were then subjected to the horrors of the 65-mile Bataan Death March, where thousands died or were executed by their captors. Thousands more Americans died on Japanese "death ships" or in brutal prisoner-of-war camps. Of the Gallup area men who were members of the "Battling Bastards of Bataan," only about half survived the nearly four-year ordeal. From left to right, Gallup brothers Dan, Nick, William, and Joe Burrola pose for a photograph in this undated photograph. William and Joe both survived the Bataan Death March. (Courtesy of the Burrola family.)

Navajo Code Talkers

When the Navajo Code Talkers returned to the United States from their tour of duty at the end of World War II, there were no parades or welcome receptions. At the time, Native Americans did not even have the right to vote in Arizona and New Mexico. It would be 23 years before the Navajo Code Talkers were finally able to tell their families, friends, fellow Marines, and the American public what they had done to help win the war. In 1968, declassification finally allowed these brave Marines to tell the story of how they had developed, written, memorized, implemented, and then passed vital information in code using the Navajo language—in real time, under battle conditions—and how vital it was to the war effort. The passing of information by code was crucial to winning many of the bloodiest battles in the Pacific theater during World War II. The original 29 recruits developed the code as a group, with leaders emerging to guide the work. Subsequent recruits would add to the code to keep it constantly changing, and more than 400 Navajo men ultimately served as Navajo Code Talkers. The code they developed, based on the Diné language, was never broken by the Japanese. The irony is that the Navajo men, recruited from the reservation and border towns like Gallup, had, in many instances, come from boarding schools where they had been punished for using their Navajo language. After declassification in 1968, public acclaim for the Navajo Marines grew. A letter of recognition from Pres. Richard Nixon was presented to the code talkers at the Navajo Tribal Fair in 1971, Pres. Ronald Reagan designated August 14, 1982, as National Navajo Code Talker Day, and the Pentagon hosted an exhibit honoring them in 1992. Pres. George W. Bush presented gold medals to the original 29 Marines in 2001, with silver medals to the code talkers who followed. There have since been many books, documentaries, and movies that have explored the story of the Navajo Code Talkers. Pictured in 2005 are Navajo Code Talkers in Monument Valley. (Courtesy of Kenji Kawano.)

Chester Nez (1923–2014)

One of the original 29 Navajo Code Talkers, Chester Nez grew up south of Gallup. In his 2012 memoir, *Code Talker: The First and Only Memoir by One of the Original Navajo Code Talkers of WWII,* Nez describes the harsh conditions of his childhood, growing up without running water, electricity, or heat. At the same time, Nez grew up protected by the love, community, language, and culture of his extended family. His childhood equipped him with the physical and mental toughness to survive the bleak years at boarding school, sometimes marked by hunger and humiliation. Like many of the other Navajo Code Talkers, Nez endured a school system that had forbidden him to speak Navajo and had been intent on eradicating his native language. This c. 1945 photograph shows Chester Nez at the Tuba City Trading Post. (Courtesy of Michael Nez.)

Hershey Miyamura (1925–)
As a kid growing up in Gallup in the late 1930s, Hiroshi "Hershey" Miyamura liked to box. He would wear a pair of boxing gloves around his neck and challenge people to fights in the alley between the O.K. Café on Coal Avenue and the Eagle Café on Route 66. In his typical self-effacing manner, Miyamura says, "I just enjoyed it, but I didn't enjoy training, so I never amounted to anything." On April 24, 1951, during the Korean War, a battle came Corporal Miyamura's way that would bring him international fame. When his squad was in a defensive position in Korea, it was overrun by Chinese troops. Miyamura first wielded a bayonet in hand-to-hand combat and then fought his way to a machine gun placement where he delivered fire into the enemy's charge. Miyamura ordered his troops to fall back while he remained to cover their retreat. Although severely wounded, when he was last seen, Miyamura was fighting alone against an overwhelming number of enemy soldiers. After 28 months as a prisoner of war in North Korea, Miyamura was one of the last US prisoners to be released. He said he realized he was back on the American side when he saw an American flag fluttering in the breeze. "That's one of the most beautiful sights I ever saw," he recalled. Miyamura learned that while he had been a prisoner, he was awarded the Congressional Medal of Honor. He said that the general who told him about the award said, "Our government kept it secret because they were afraid of retaliation from the enemy because of what you did." Before being presented with the Medal of Honor by Pres. Dwight D. Eisenhower in Washington, DC, Miyamura was met in San Francisco by his parents and wife, who brought him back to Gallup for a surprise welcome by the entire town. After the Korean War, Hershey and Tsuruko "Terry" Miyamura (1925–2014) raised their children in Gallup, where he worked at a service station on the west end of Gallup that he co-owned. Gallup honored Miyamura, the city's most celebrated war hero, by naming a high school after him. (Courtesy of the National Archives, photograph No. 111-LC34233.)

Annie Dodge Wauneka (1910–1997)

Born in 1910, Annie Dodge Wauneka was the youngest daughter of Henry Chee Dodge, the first chairman of the Navajo Nation Tribal Council. She was elected to the tribal council in 1951, where she became the second woman member. Sent to a boarding school at eight years old, Wauneka survived the deadly 1918 Spanish Influenza epidemic during her first school year. Wauneka stayed to help the nurse care for the other children, and this experience sparked her lifelong interest in public health. In 1963, Pres. John F. Kennedy's administration announced that Wauneka was a recipient of the Presidential Medal of Freedom Award. After Kennedy's assassination, Wauneka received the award from Pres. Lyndon B. Johnson. At the time, Wauneka was one of only 21 Americans to have been awarded the medal, and the first Native American recipient. Wauneka also received an honorary doctorate in humanities (public health) from the University of New Mexico. She worked tirelessly on behalf of the Diné people to improve conditions on the reservation, particularly championing health care and education improvements. She was a leader in the fight to eradicate tuberculosis in the Navajo Nation, and served as a translator and educator for improving health practices. Appointed chair of the Navajo Tribal Council's Health and Welfare Committee, Wauneka tackled other issues including water quality, alcoholism, and infant mortality. Wauneka was among a number of Navajo speakers who hosted educational and informational programs on Gallup radio station KGAK. Her father had insisted education was a key to improving life on the reservation, and Wauneka continued to promote that work all her life. In 1984, the Navajo Tribal Council honored Wauneka by naming her "Legendary Mother of the Navajo People." Wauneka died at the age of 87, after years of public service and countless awards. Wauneka is the subject of and author of several books, one titled *I'll Go and Do More*, based on one of her many quotes. Wauneka was inducted into the National Women's Hall of Fame on October 7, 2000. New Mexico's Historical Marker Project erected a historical highway marker in her honor on Highway 134 in McKinley County. In this photograph, President Johnson speaks from the podium as Annie Dodge Wauneka is presented with the Medal of Freedom. (Photograph by Cecil Stoughton, courtesy of LBJ Presidential Library.)

Emmett Garcia (1938–2011)

Gallup mayor Emmett "Frankie" Garcia was elected to a two-year term as mayor in 1971. Garcia was a 35-year-old rising political star who had been shaking things up in Gallup. He came into office early, stayed late, and pushed his staff hard with a steady stream of ideas and projects. He actively sought a large federal grant for an alcohol rehabilitation program. In February 1973, Gov. Bruce King offered Garcia one of the most prized political appointments in New Mexico—a seat on the University of New Mexico (UNM) Board of Regents. The appointment came at a difficult time for Garcia, and he first suggested another Gallupian for the position. However, Garcia relented when the governor's son told him the appointment would go outside Gallup if he did not accept it. Garcia, who was facing reelection in March, was going through a series of misfortunes. Just after New Year's Day, his ailing wife was diagnosed with lupus. Although she would go on to live for years, at the time doctors told Garcia she only had weeks to live. In February, Garcia survived a head-on collision in Arizona and was left bruised, beaten up, and hobbling on crutches. When Garcia's appointment to the regents went before the Rules Committee of the New Mexico State Senate, Gallup resident Larry Casuse appeared and spoke in opposition, citing Garcia's ownership interest in the Navajo Inn bar on the doorstep of the Navajo Reservation. Garcia acknowledged he had a one-third ownership interest, but said he did not have an active role in the bar's management. Casuse and others protested when Garcia took a seat on the Board of Regents on February 23, 1973. One week later, Garcia was kidnapped at gunpoint from city hall by Casuse and an accomplice and marched to a sporting goods store on Route 66. With his arms handcuffed behind him, Garcia kicked Casuse's accomplice and dove through a glass door. Garcia was hit in the back by a spray of shotgun pellets as he ran toward the door. Casuse died of gunshot wounds in the ensuing standoff. Garcia, who had been strongly favored to win reelection before the controversy and kidnapping, lost his bid for reelection. He bought out his two partners in the Navajo Inn, which lost its lease and then was closed and bulldozed. Shortly thereafter, Garcia moved from Gallup to Arizona. Garcia, center, is shown with former political rivals Pete Derizotis, left, and Earl Stewart. (Courtesy of the Bob Rosebrough Collection.)

Larry Casuse (1952–1973)

Larry Casuse was in high school when his family moved to Gallup from Silver City. His father, a Navajo man from Mexican Springs, and his mother, an Austrian, met in Germany after World War II. Intellectually curious, Casuse was always reading a book growing up. In Gallup, he played football for Gallup High School and took up wrestling. His closest friends were other Navajo football players, and he was active in the Indian Club, which held Gallup High's first powwow. In college, Casuse joined UNM's Kiva Club and was elected president. He joined protests of Gallup's Inter-Tribal Indian Ceremonial, which he viewed as being exploitive of Native artists. Just before Casuse's sophomore year at UNM, tragedy struck his life when he hit and killed a young Navajo woman who walked out on the highway north of Gallup late at night. Casuse was charged with leaving the scene of an accident involving death. His lawyer waived a jury trial, and Casuse was convicted in a trial before a judge. Casuse then obtained a new lawyer who successfully sought a new trial by jury. That resulted in a mistrial when the jury deadlocked 11-1 in favor of conviction. With a third trial scheduled, Casuse felt the prosecution was politically motivated to punish him for his activism. At the same time, he began actively protesting the appointment of Gallup mayor Emmett Garcia to the UNM Board of Regents. Casuse appeared before a state senate committee and the Board of Regents and argued that Garcia was unfit because he was a co-owner of a problem bar on the reservation border. On March 1, 1973, one week after Garcia took office as a regent and two days after American Indian Movement activists began their occupation of Wounded Knee, South Dakota, Casuse and an accomplice kidnapped Garcia at city hall and marched him at gunpoint to a sporting goods store on Route 66. Law enforcement officers responded en masse. After a brief standoff and Garcia's escape, Casuse died in the ensuing fusillade. Over 3,000 people, mostly Navajo, attended Casuse's funeral, and later, thousands marched in the streets of Gallup in memory of Casuse. The circumstances of his death are still controversial. Some believe Casuse took his own life, and others believe he was killed by police while trying to surrender. In the spring of 2017, memorial posters featuring Casuse's image began appearing in Gallup after city officials removed a downtown planter with a similar image, a move that generated controversy in the community. (Courtesy of Chuck Van Drunen.)

Edward Munoz (1927–2006)

Edward "Eddie" Munoz started school without knowing how to speak English and later said that he got spanked a lot for speaking Spanish. Munoz had a little red wagon, and after school, he delivered clothes his mother laundered and tamales she cooked. At 16, he lied about his age to enlist in the Merchant Marines during World War II. After the war, Munoz and a group of other "Young Turks" dived into Gallup politics. Munoz's incredibly forceful and determined personality made success inevitable. He became Gallup's longest tenured mayor and served terms from 1958 to 1969 and from 1987 to 1991. Between his terms as mayor, Munoz, influenced by his wife and daughter, Margaret and Connie, became active in a charismatic Christian church, and he decided to tackle Gallup's longstanding alcohol problems. When Munoz was in the service, his father had been hit and killed by a drunk driver, and his brother was hit and killed by a state police car while he was walking across Route 66 after drinking. Munoz had also lost a close friend to alcoholism. During Munoz's second stint as mayor, the city shut down the long-overcrowded drunk tank and replaced it with a detox center, and by referendum vote, banned Sunday liquor sales. Munoz worked in tandem with administrators at Rehoboth McKinley Christian Hospital in 1989 to plan the Journey for Jovita March to Santa Fe to seek alcohol reforms. The march was named after a local baby who died after her family's vehicle was struck by a drunk driver. Munoz walked every step of the 215-mile march. At night, he cut his socks off and bandaged his bloody feet. The group of walkers swelled over the course of the march to include thousands on the final day and prompted a recalcitrant legislature to pass laws to ban drive-up liquor windows and impose a five-percent liquor tax to fund alcohol treatment. Several of Munoz's alcohol reform initiatives, which were originally proposed only for Gallup, were eventually adopted statewide. Munoz narrowly escaped a recall election that was generated by backlash from the negative publicity that his efforts drew to Gallup's problems with alcohol abuse. Munoz, far right, is shown in this *Santa Fe New Mexican* photograph taken by Larry Beckner. (Courtesy of the Palace of the Governors Photo Archives, NMHM/DCA, No. HP.2014.14.744.)

James B. Lewis (1947–)

A star athlete at Gallup High School in the 1960s, James B. Lewis built a career as a respected New Mexico public servant. In 1982, Lewis ran for the office of Bernalillo County treasurer even though he had been told an African American man could not win a county-wide race. Lewis won and received more votes than anyone else on the Democratic county ticket that year. Appointed state treasurer in 1985, Lewis ran for a full term in 1986, becoming the first African American person elected to a statewide office. He went on to serve as chief of staff for Gov. Bruce King, city administrator of Rio Rancho, assistant secretary of the Department of Energy, and chief administrative officer of Albuquerque. In 2006 and 2010, Lewis won two more terms as state treasurer. (Courtesy of James B. Lewis.)

Joel Jasperse (1953–)
When former Rehoboth High School English teacher Joel Jasperse decided to attend UNM Law School in 1978, he had no idea that decision would one day lead him to argue a case before the US Supreme Court. As an attorney for Gallup's New Mexico Legal Aid office, Jasperse contested the Indian Health Service's (IHS) decision to shut down a program to diagnose and treat disabled Native children. Jasperse won in US District Court when the judge ordered IHS to reinstate the program and the US 10th Circuit Court of Appeals affirmed that decision. In the Supreme Court, Jasperse lost the battle when the court ruled in favor of IHS but won the war when IHS continued to offer the program for many more years. Jasperse has worked for more than 30 years to help poor citizens gain equal access to justice. (Courtesy of the *Gallup Independent*, Brian Leddy.)

Notable Newsmakers

A number of individuals who have enjoyed high-profile careers in sports, entertainment, science, and other fields have ties to Gallup. Here are just a few.

Adopted and raised by a Gallup family, Tom Bee became a recording artist, songwriter, and music producer. Bee founded the Native American rock group XIT, which provided the soundtrack for much of the American Indian Movement political activism of the 1970s.

The Boston Red Sox gained untold numbers of local fans when Jacoby Ellsbury, who is half Navajo, became the Sox's center fielder in 2007. He then broke their hearts when he joined the New York Yankees in 2014. Ellsbury, who was not raised locally, has relatives in Gallup.

Born in Gallup, Mike G. Everitt graduated from high school in Aztec, New Mexico. Now a professional Major League Baseball (MLB) umpire, Everitt can frequently be seen on television umpiring MLB regular season and playoff games.

One of contemporary Christian music's most successful singer/songwriters, Rich Mullins spent the last years of his life in the Gallup area. When not traveling on tour, Mullins and fellow musician Mitch McVickers lived in hogans they built near Window Rock.

A noted astronomer and award-winning scientist, Carolyn Spellmann Shoemaker was born in Gallup. She is a codiscoverer of Comet Shoemaker–Levy 9 and is renowned for her expertise in discovering comets and asteroids.

Ballet dancer Jock Soto was born in Gallup to a Navajo mother and a Puerto Rican father. Raised in Phoenix, Soto was admitted into New York City's School of American Ballet at age 12. During his career, he rose to become the principal dancer at the New York City Ballet.

Born in Italy, Giovanni Zavatti was brought to Gallup by his father to work as a coal miner. Zavatti, who had been accepted into the Vatican's boys' choir, resisted that destiny and pursued his dream to become an opera singer, which he did. His story is told in the Youtube video "Giovanni Zavatti, Tenor: In His Own Words."

J. René Peña has built a successful professional acting career featuring many theater, film, television, and commercial credits. Locally, however, the Gallup native is known for *Traveling with Angels*, the one-woman play she wrote after her husband died of cancer in 2010. Pictured is J. René Peña. (Courtesy of the *Gallup Independent*, Cable Hoover.)

Mother Teresa (1910–1997)

Mother Teresa, now St. Teresa of Calcutta, visited Gallup twice and established ministries for her Missionaries of Charity here. Her sisters operate a soup kitchen and shelter on Gallup's north side and have assisted with the ministry at St. Patrick's Mission south of town. During her visit in 1988, Mother Teresa was asked if she saw a special need in Gallup. "There is just as much need here as in New York, as in Washington, as in Calcutta," she replied. "Different needs. Here they may not need what they need in Africa, but everywhere there's a need, there's a need for love." A step stool was provided for the diminutive Mother Teresa when she spoke to the standing-room-only crowd at Sacred Heart Cathedral. (Courtesy of Martin Link, 1988.)

CHAPTER TWO

Traders and Native Culture

The history of Indian traders in Gallup and surrounding reservation communities includes the names of some of the most famous and influential trading families, both in the formative years and in modern times, names like Cotton, Tanner, Turpen, Richardson, Foutz, Wallace, Burnham, Hubbell, and Ortega. The complex dynamics involved in the relationship between Indian traders and the Native American community cannot be overstated. Early trading posts were not only general stores, they were also post offices, banking establishments, and community gathering places, and they were places marked by a cultural exchange that unfolded over decades. After the Diné people returned to their homeland following the Long Walk, traders provided a wide range of goods to remote communities on the reservation. Early traders became fluent in Native languages and, in some cases, married into the local community and became in-laws. Native Americans relied on traders to provide them with basic goods, to get them through lean times, and to help with sick family members. They learned English and learned more about their non-Indian neighbors, for better or worse. Many of these relationships have lasted generations. Some Native elders have never used a banking institution; rather, they have preferred to store their valuables, usually jewelry and saddles, as pawn at a trusted trading post.

In Gallup, as on the nearby Navajo Nation and Pueblo of Zuni, Indian traders have been instrumental in creating and marketing the demand for Native American arts and crafts. Also in Gallup, Indian traders were instrumental in the founding of the Inter-Tribal Indian Ceremonial. The Inter-Tribal Indian Ceremonial was created not only to showcase the culture of various Native American tribes, but also to increase public interest in Native arts and crafts and bring more tourist dollars to the region. Both the Indian trading system and the Gallup Inter-Tribal Indian Ceremonial have not been without their critics, especially during the activist years of the 1960s and 1970s. However, just as Indian traders and their trading posts have evolved through the decades, the local Native American community has changed. More Native American people are entering the arts-and-crafts business as business owners, and more are assuming leadership roles in Gallup's Ceremonial. Those developments, gradual though they may be, are helping to transform Gallup's tourist slogan, "The Indian Capital of the World," into a more authentic description of the city's Native cultural heritage.

Tanner Family, Five Generations of Indian Traders

John Tanner (1778–1850), a prominent businessman from Upstate New York, gifted his estate to the Church of Jesus Christ of Latter-day Saints (LDS) after a miracle cure of an injured leg. He then joined Joseph Smith for the trek west, and his sons were instrumental in all phases of the migration. Son Seth Tanner (1828–1918) found his totem *Shush*, or Bear, on the move farther west to Salt Lake City with the prophet Brigham Young. His family traveled to Navajo land to settle Tuba City, Arizona, where they built their homestead and started the first Tanner Trading Post in 1872. Sent by the LDS Church on various expeditions around the American Southwest, Seth Tanner found and established Tanner Trail near the Grand Canyon, Tanner Crossing at the Little Colorado River, and Tanner Wash. Of Seth Tanner's seven children, his son Joseph Baldwin "J.B." Tanner (1868–1944) played a prominent role in the Southwest Indian trading and jewelry business. Like many of the traders, Tanner, who was given the Navajo name *Shush Yaz* or Little Bear, spoke several Native languages but was fluent in Navajo. He led a number of domestic turquoise mining expeditions and was responsible for much of the importing of Mediterranean coral and Persian turquoise around the turn of the 20th century. Tanner was instrumental in the marriage of silver and turquoise, providing local Native American talent with these quality materials and cultivating strong relationships between Navajo artisans and the Tanner family. Joseph Baldwin had 13 children with his wife, Nora Foutz, many of whom stayed in the trade. One son, Ruel Lehi Tanner (1899–1957), had eight children, seven of whom led trading careers across the Southwest. The Tanner family has sold and traded in almost every facet of Native American arts and culture, including wool and mohair, specialty folk art, livestock, saddles, Bluebird flour, pinon nuts, pottery, weavings, jewelry, and turquoise. The tradition continues today. In Gallup, Ruel Tanner's sons have been heavily involved in the Indian art business. The late J.B. Tanner (1924–2008) and Don Tanner (1932–2007) were both longtime traders here. Ellis Tanner of Ellis Tanner Trading Company and Joe Tanner of Tanners Indian Art continue to operate successful Gallup businesses. Joe Tanner, along with his wife, Cindy, and daughter Emerald, represents the fifth generation of Tanner traders with their downtown Gallup gallery. Joseph Baldwin Tanner is pictured. (Courtesy of the Tanner family.)

Clinton Neal Cotton (1859–1936)
C.N. Cotton arrived in the Gallup area in 1881 as a telegrapher for the Atlantic & Pacific Railroad, but soon became one of the region's most influential Indian traders, as well as Gallup businessman, banker, and mayor. Cotton struck up a friendship with Manuelito, and when the Navajo leader died, Cotton hired Chicago sculptor Herman McNeil to create a towering statue of Manuelito. Cotton placed the statue in an exterior niche at his large trading warehouse, located at Third Street and the railroad tracks, where it overlooked the downtown and became a Gallup landmark. In recent years, the sculpture was donated to McKinley County by businessman Joe DiGregorio. It has since been restored and now stands at the entrance to the courthouse rotunda, once again a community landmark. (Courtesy of Octavia Fellin Public Library.)

Ceremonial Founders

Gallup's first Inter-Tribal Indian Ceremonial began in September 1922. The idea was proposed by Kiwanis Club members but is usually credited to Mike Kirk, who was said to have sold Ceremonial as a way to promote more tourism to Gallup as the heart of Indian Country. It was also promoted as a way to showcase a variety of Native American arts, crafts, and dance in one central location. Skeptics, including influential businessman and trader C.N. Cotton, were not convinced it would work. It took all of Kirk's persuasive powers to find the Native American participants as well. With traders Ray Aldrich, Evon Zartman Vogt Sr., J.B. Tanner, Roman Hubbell, and others on board, the community got behind the idea. For the first Ceremonial, Mayor Steve Vidal declared a holiday so citizens could help build the campgrounds and grandstands. Locals managed to get the first event off the ground in just five weeks. In the early days, Native American families traveled to Gallup with horses and wagons and camped out in the surrounding hills. Tourists from across the nation braved dirt roads in their newly acquired automobiles to get to Gallup to purchase Native arts and crafts and view traditional Indian dances that had seldom been performed for the public. Early Ceremonial events included buffalo riding, horse racing, apple bobbing, women's tug-of-wars, a cross-country race, and spectator participation in social dancing. In 1974, Ceremonial was moved from its traditional grounds on the north side of Gallup to scenic Red Rock Park because of the construction of Interstate 40. Today, the Gallup Inter-Tribal Indian Ceremonial is considered the city's signature event. As it approaches its 100th anniversary, Ceremonial is one of the oldest continuous events in the state, and one of the largest Native American gatherings in the country. The Gallup Inter-Tribal Indian Ceremonial Board of Directors is pictured in the early 1930s. (Courtesy of the Octavia Fellin Public Library.)

Della Casa-Appa (1889–1963)
One of the first significant female jewelers in Zuni Pueblo, Della Casa-Appa challenged tradition when she began assisting her jeweler husband. She then moved on to creating artwork in her own name. Today, female artists are well represented as jewelry makers in Zuni Pueblo and other tribes. In this painting by Jim Abeita, Casa-Appa wears her famous squash blossom necklace. (Courtesy of Tanner Indian Arts.)

Boyd Jones (1914–1970)
In 1928, Boyd Jones was a 14-year-old local cowboy with a big idea. In an effort to publicize Gallup's Inter-Tribal Indian Ceremonial, Jones rode 1,800 miles by horseback from Gallup to Wisconsin, home of Pres. Calvin Coolidge's Summer White House, to personally invite the president to the Ceremonial. Coolidge did not attend, but the teenager received national media coverage. (Courtesy of Octavia Fellin Public Library, W.T. Mullarky.)

Zuni Olla Maidens (c. 1922)
For more than 90 years, the Zuni Olla Maidens have been a favorite of audiences at the Gallup Inter-Tribal Indian Ceremonial. By balancing ollas on their heads while they dance in traditional Zuni regalia, the women honor their ancestral grandmothers who similarly hauled precious water to care for their families. Each woman places small bags of salt from the Zuni Salt Lake and cornmeal in their olla and then breaths in a blessing from their pot before placing it on their head. The dance group has performed across the country and has been featured in the documentary *Singing Our Stories*. Also honored by New Mexico's Historical Marker Project, the group's roadside marker is located on New Mexico State Route 53, just east of Zuni Pueblo. (Both, courtesy of the *Gallup Independent*, Cable Hoover.)

Dwight D. Eisenhower (1890–1969)
With its location along the railroad and interstate highway, Gallup has attracted its share of presidential candidates stumping for votes. During his campaign tour through the Southwest, Dwight D. Eisenhower stopped in Gallup for the Ceremonial on August 10, 1952. Eisenhower, pictured with Native American dignitaries and L.E. "Bobcat" Wilson, promoted his support for Native American voting rights. (Courtesy of the City of Gallup, Ceremonial Collection, W.T. Mullarky.)

Narciso Abeyta (1918–1998)
Renowned Navajo artist Narciso Abeyta trained at Dorothy Dunn's Studio School at the Santa Fe Indian School. Dunn called him the Paul Gauguin of her studio. After serving in World War II, Narcisco married Sylvia Shipley, a Quaker from Pennsylvania. The couple moved to Gallup, where they raised seven children, including daughter Pablita, a sculptor, and son Tony, an acclaimed contemporary artist. (Courtesy of Tony Abeyta.)

Bill Richardson (1919–2017)

One would need a genealogy chart and a map of the Navajo Nation to identify all the traders in the Richardson family and the location of all the trading posts that provided Bill Richardson with the DNA, the training and experience, and just plain old know-how to successfully build Richardson's Trading Company into one of the most highly respected trading businesses in the region. In fact, there is a book written by family member Gladwell Richardson, titled *Navajo Trader*, that describes the complex legacy. Except for the time Richardson was in Texas during World War II, he spent his entire career working as a trader to the Diné people. Prior to running Richardson's Trading Company in Gallup, Richardson worked at 18 trading posts owned by various family members in remote locations on the Navajo Reservation in Arizona. Generations of customers from the Navajo Nation continue to patronize Richardson's Gallup store, which is a working pawn shop where rugs, jewelry, saddles, and family heirlooms are pawned for safekeeping and usually only redeemed for religious or important social events. Richardson's Trading is also an important tourist highlight on Gallup's main street, Historic Route 66, where one can purchase authentic handmade Native American art. Into his late 90s, Richardson could still be found at his desk daily, regaling anyone who stopped by with entertaining stories. There was the tale about George McAdams, the first in his line of Navajo traders, who was a gambler and had to leave New Mexico because he found himself on the wrong side of the law. And then there were stories of Henry Chee Dodge, the first chairman of the Navajo Tribe, who was also on the board of directors of Gallup's First State Bank; Dodge used to hold court at the park across the street from Richardson's Trading, promoting the importance of education to a group of young Navajo men. Richardson and Richardson's Trading Company are now interwoven in the culture of Gallup and its long history of Native American art and trading posts. (Courtesy of the *Gallup Independent*, Cable Hoover.)

Bill Malone (1939–) and Minnie Goodluck Malone (1937–)
Minnie Goodluck Malone, a third-generation Navajo weaver, grew up learning to weave from her grandmother May Smith and mother, Mary Smith-Avery. As a young girl, she would weave on her grandmother's loom and then unweave her work until it met her grandmother's approval. She met her husband, Bill Malone, when she brought her first rug into the Lupton, Arizona, trading post where he was working as a trader for the first time. The couple then spent 20 years in Pinon, Arizona—Minnie as postmaster and Bill as trader—and then 24 years at the famed Hubbell Trading Post in Ganado, Arizona. Minnie, also an accomplished jeweler, continues to weave, and Bill now operates his own business, Bill Malone Trading, which opened in downtown Gallup in 2012. (Both, courtesy of Bill Malone.)

Chester Kahn (1936–) and Ellis Tanner (1943–)

The murals of artist Chester Kahn (above) are some of Gallup's most beautiful artistic gems. Named "Ceremonial Living Legend" in 2008, Kahn's work includes his monumental *Circle of Light* murals at Ellis Tanner Trading Company, shown in this photograph, which took seven years to complete; his *Native American Trading* mural downtown; and 36 murals in Gallup's El Rancho Hotel. Indian trader Ellis Tanner has been a trailblazer in promoting appreciation for Native American culture and history. He opened a Navajo bookstore in his trading business and commissioned Chester Kahn to paint the *Circle of Light* murals in order to provide Navajo youth with inspiring and positive role models. For several years, Tanner (below) sponsored his own Native American Appreciation Day, which he hoped the city would continue. (Both, courtesy of the *Gallup Independent*, Nicole Goodhue.)

Jim Abeita (1947–)
Gallup painter Jim Abeita credits his uncle Joe with being his first art teacher. The two of them would etch drawings into rocks during long days watching sheep graze in the hills near Crownpoint, New Mexico. Abeita also credits Duane Berg, his Gallup High School art teacher, with helping him show and sell his work at the Gallup Inter-Tribal Indian Ceremonial, and Gallup photographer and businessman Nello T. Guadagnoli, of Mullarky Studios, for helping promote his artwork. But Abeita says it was his first wife, Hannah, who really was the person who made his career happen. After Abeita finished studying at the American Academy of Art in Chicago, Hannah started marketing his work. As his advocate and salesperson, she started taking his paintings around to galleries in Chicago. Abeita describes the time Hannah took his painting of country music star Johnny Cash to a concert and pushed her way forward to a meeting with the legendary "Man in Black" himself. This encounter resulted in Abeita being granted a three-month residence in Nashville at Cash's estate, where Abeita painted everyone in the extended family and established a lasting friendship with them. Abeita also painted cover art for a Cash album, and met many of country music's royalty and painted them too. In 1976, Abeita had a book published, titled *American Indians of Abeita: His People,* which had been a dream of Hannah's. Tragically, she died in a car crash before it was published. Johnny Cash wrote the dedication in the book to Hannah, and he also wrote the song *Navajo*, which he said was inspired by Abeita and includes references to Gallup and Crownpoint. Abeita, known for his realism style of painting, broke from the stylized, two-dimensional Native American painting style that was taught by Dorothy Dunn at the Santa Fe Indian School. As a result, Abeita has inspired many Native artists to follow suit and paint in styles and media of their own choosing. Abeita's paintings—rich in imagery, humor, tradition, history, and detail—are highly sought after by collectors around the world. Abeita was named the Gallup Inter-Tribal Indian Ceremonial's 2006 Living Treasure. This self-portrait was done by Jim Abeita and is in the collection of his daughter Sheila. (Photograph of painting courtesy of the *Gallup Independent.*)

Raymond Yazzie (1960–) and Colina Yazzie (1959–)
Colina Gorman met Raymond Yazzie when he walked into her workplace, Ganado's famous Hubbell Trading Post. The two came from families of artisans. Colina was from a family of weavers and jewelry makers, and Raymond was from a family of celebrated jewelers, in which three of the siblings have garnered international recognition, including an exhibition of their art titled "The Glittering World" at the Smithsonian National Museum of the American Indian. In 1994, Colina and Raymond opened Yazzie's Indian Arts in Gallup, the first completely Navajo-owned Native arts business downtown. They have continued to select and market pieces to showcase the diversity and beauty of all forms of Native American artwork, which includes Colina's beaded necklaces, Raymond's jewelry, and exquisite examples of other art such as paintings, sculpture, and clothing. (Photograph by Carol Sarath.)

Theresa Fraizer (1961–)
Of Laguna, Hopi, and Chippewa heritage, Fraizer is the fourth generation of her family to participate in the Gallup Inter-Tribal Indian Ceremonial. First a dancer and then a board member, Fraizer served as executive director of the Ceremonial from 2009 to 2012. She also organizes Gallup's Nightly Indian Dances, popular with tourists and residents alike, which take place from Memorial Day to Labor Day. (Courtesy of Theresa Fraizer.)

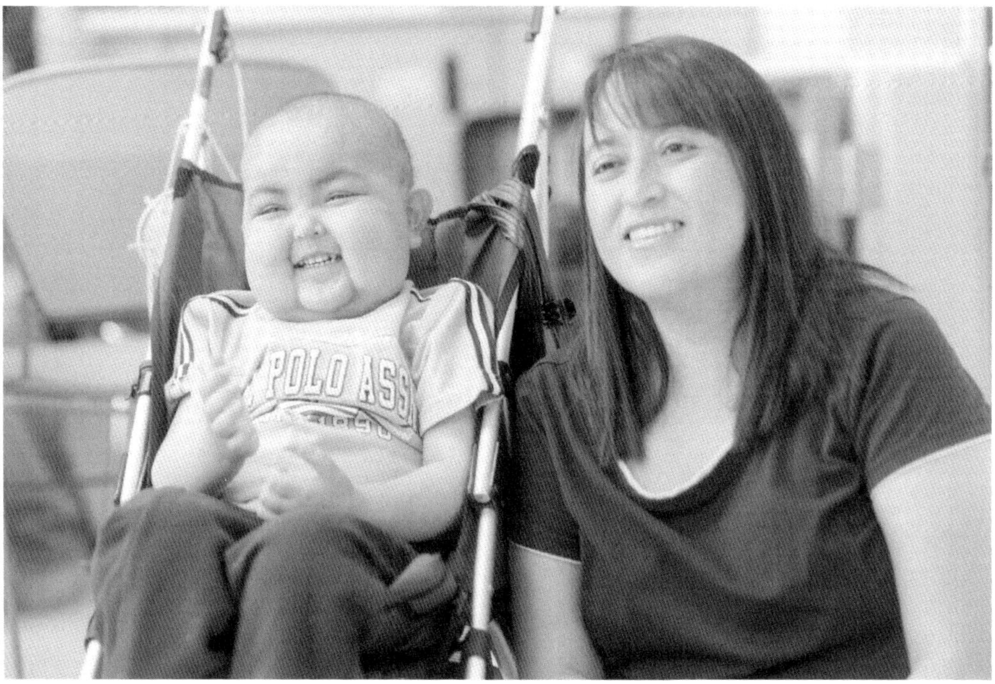

Hilda Bowman (1962–)
Hilda Bowman stepped into the Inter-Tribal Indian Ceremonial office as a volunteer and onto the board with the goal of seeing Ceremonial reach its 100th anniversary. Like many longtime Gallup residents, Bowman has fond childhood memories of Ceremonial. She recalls how families traveled into Gallup on horses and wagons, and she remembers being frightened by the Apache Crown Dancers. Hilda is seen with her late son Nicholas. (Courtesy of Hilda Bowman.)

Aaron Bryant Anderson (1970–)
Award-winning artist Aaron Anderson (above) is a third-generation Navajo jeweler who grew up in Gallup, learning the art from family members. His grandfather, Bryant Anderson (left), was an esteemed jeweler. Anderson remembers his mother, Evelyn, creating jewelry to support the family as a single mother before she earned her degree and began her career as a teacher. Anderson credits his stepfather, Wilford Henry, with reintroducing jewelry-making into his life. Anderson took all these lessons and used them to create unique art pieces crafted from a technique called tufa casting. Anderson has said that, with his business, he wants to prove to all Native artists that Gallup is a place where they can make and market their art and be successful. (Above, courtesy of *Turquoise Skies*, TSkies.com; left, courtesy of Aaron Anderson.)

CHAPTER THREE

Community Builders

In observations about Gallup, Pastor Jay McCollum of Gallup's First Baptist Church once said, "You've got to have a little grit in your gizzard to live here." Although humans do not have gizzards, his point is well taken. Gallup is sometimes a tough little town to live in, and it takes a special type of person to not only carve out a satisfying life here, but to also thrive and flourish.

It has been that way since Gallup was founded. As a rough, Western railroad town, Gallup sprang up along the rail lines with dirt roads, wooden sidewalks, barrooms, and brothels. It would take a number of determined citizens to begin the hard work of turning wild and woolly Gallup into a family-friendly community full of successful schools, businesses, hospitals, houses of worship, and civic organizations. It is an ongoing challenge, but each new generation makes Gallup a better place to live.

A common theme in the lives of the individuals profiled in this chapter is service to the community. Many of these citizens have dedicated professional careers or untold hours of volunteer labor to building businesses, giving back to the community, serving in government, caring for others, working in religious ministries, creating opportunities for children, advocating for justice, providing needed services, establishing nonprofit organizations, educating students, beautifying the environment, improving recreational activities, inspiring kids—in other words, leaving Gallup a better place than when they began.

Another theme is the number of outstanding individuals who have left indelible contributions. Evon Zartman Vogt was a modern-day Renaissance man whose early work at El Morro National Monument continues to bring visitors from around the world to the region. Under an appointment by Pres. Dwight D. Eisenhower, Gallup banker Glenn L. Emmons rose to become commissioner of the Bureau of Indian Affairs. Geronimo Martin and Faye Edgerton created a lasting legacy for Navajo Christians. Octavia Fellin built Gallup's wonderful library, and Sally Noe researched and preserved local history. Armand Ortega saved the iconic El Rancho Hotel and restored it to its previous beauty, and Dr. Bruce Tempest helped solve a medical mystery and save lives. And because of passionate hobbyists like Alan Wilson and the founders of the Red Rock Balloon Rally, every December, people of Gallup can marvel at the beauty of colorful hot-air balloons gliding over spectacular Red Rock Park.

Librada Montoya Fellin (1896–1991)
The first nurse at Gallup's early hospital, located in the Victorian stone house on South Second Street, Librada Montoya Fellin, shown here with her husband, Otto, was the daughter of Gallup settlers Candelario and Juanita Montoya. Trained as a nurse in Albuquerque, Fellin's nursing diploma was signed by pioneering physician Dr. William Randolph Lovelace. The mother of seven children, Fellin later worked for many years at St. Mary's Hospital. (Courtesy of Leonard Fellin.)

Evon Zartman Vogt Sr. (1880–1943)
Evon Zartman Vogt Sr. came to New Mexico as a young man after being diagnosed with tuberculosis. The Vogt Ranch House in Ramah, which is now listed in the National Register of Historic Places, became a gathering place for visiting writers, artists, historians, and anthropologists. Vogt, the first custodian of El Morro National Monument, founded the *Gallup Gazette* newspaper. He is pictured here in 1938 with Yazzie Pino and family. (Courtesy of the Vogt descendants.)

George K. Taira (1883–1959) and Glenn L. Emmons (1895–1980)

A native of Japan, George K. Taira (left) moved to Gallup in 1920 and became a prominent leader of the local Japanese American community. As an owner of the Eagle Café, Taira became friends with Glenn L. Emmons (below) of First State Bank. Although almost none of Gallup's Japanese American citizens were removed to internment camps during World War II, their cameras, radios, and firearms were confiscated. According to Taira's daughter Kay, their bank accounts were also frozen. Emmons intervened on Taira's behalf, sparing his home from search, and he transferred Taira's money into his own bank account so Taira could continue to do business. After one local man was placed in an internment camp, Taira organized the Japanese American community to financially support the man's family. In 1953, Emmons was tapped by Pres. Dwight D. Eisenhower to become commissioner of the Bureau of Indian Affairs. (Left, courtesy of the Taira family; below, courtesy of the *Gallup Independent*.)

Enrico Menapace (1893–1971)

Enrico Menapace's parents immigrated to Gallup from Europe's Tyrol region, which at the time was under Austrian rule but is now part of northern Italy. Menapace's first business was selling sausage from a wagon he hauled around as a 12-year-old boy. An exceptional card player, Menapace won his first real money during World War I playing poker when he drove a commanding officer around. When he returned to Gallup, Menapace built Rico Motors by borrowing money on a handshake, pooled with his poker winnings. Menapace was brilliant in math, spoke many languages, and was a business innovator. His daughter Lorene recalled, "The people from General Motors could not believe my dad's business because he was taking in sheep and cows and jewelry and rugs and whatever people had to make a payment." (Both, courtesy of the Menapace family.)

George Bubany (1890–1966)

As a young man, George Bubany lost his fingers on his left hand and part of his thumb. He also spoke with a distinct accent and was a famously terrible driver. Once, as the story goes, tourists mistook Bubany for a panhandler when he took off his hat and was holding it with the stub of his thumb and swiping his brow with a bandana. Yet Bubany, as an entrepreneur and mayor, accomplished as much as anyone ever has in Gallup. He started Bubany Lumber, Gallup Sand and Gravel, and Bubany Insurance—all still in business today. He was one of the founders of both Merchants Bank and Gallup Federal Saving and Loan. As city councilor and mayor, Bubany worked tirelessly to clean up the physical appearance of Gallup and fought against gambling and prostitution. (Courtesy of the collection of John Kozeliski.)

Basilio Di Gregorio (1913–2001)

Basilio Di Gregorio was one of the throngs of young immigrant men who came to Gallup to work in the coal mines and seek a better life. In 1938, he started a little grocery store where Jerry's Café is now located. Because he traveled to California to get fresh produce and Italian specialties, he named his store California Market. As his business expanded, Di Gregorio became an icon of Gallup's golden age of business. (Courtesy of Joe Di Gregorio.)

Guido Zecca Sr. (1894–1990)

After World War I, Guido Zecca Sr. was traveling back home to Arizona by train when he stopped in Gallup. He was so impressed by Gallup's turnout for the troops that he ended up staying here permanently. As a young man, Zecca wrestled the welterweight champion of the world to a draw in the biggest wrestling match Gallup has ever seen. He later went on to serve as a state senator. (Courtesy of the Zecca family.)

Clair E. Gurley (1907–2006)

Clair Gurley came to Gallup in 1932 from South Dakota and bought the Ford dealership, then called Central Motors, from a gruff old Englishman who was eager to focus his energy on coal mining. With the passage of time, it became clear that Gurley made the better choice of business pursuits. Gurley's son Pat, who would later run the company, would say, "Gurley Motor Company sold more retail Ford pickups than anybody in the US. That was back in the heyday in the early 50s." Gurley was a pillar of the community in its formative years. In 1948, he was elected to the town council and was the driving force in the construction of the present public library. Gurley also donated 59 acres to the University of New Mexico for the current site of the University of New Mexico Gallup branch (UNM-Gallup). (Courtesy of the *Gallup Independent*.)

Mary Colter (1869–1958)

A woman in a man's field, architect Mary Colter successfully raised American architecture from the shadows of Europe. Colter spent her career working with Fred Harvey and the Santa Fe Railway, designing train stations, hotels, and restaurants. Gallup's now demolished El Navajo Hotel, completed in 1923, has been called Colter's masterpiece. The hotel's design generated controversy because it featured the first permanent installation of Navajo sandpaintings. Most of El Navajo was torn down in 1957 to widen Route 66; the remaining portion of the building now houses the Gallup Cultural Center's train station, museum, and Angela's Café. Vintage photographs of Colter's stunning El Navajo are on display. (Right, courtesy of Arizona Historical Society-Pioneer Museum, Flagstaff; below, courtesy of Octavia Public Fellin Library, W.T. Mullarky.)

Mary Toki Mochimaru Montoya (1916–2015)
Local resident Mary Montoya became a Harvey Girl at Gallup's glamorous El Navajo Hotel. The daughter of Konozo and Maria Mochimaru—her father was from Japan and her mother was from Mexico—Montoya worked her way up from being a waitress at the lunch counter to running the main dining room. She later became the longtime manager of the Ranch Kitchen. (Courtesy of Rose Marie Sandoval.)

Bud Hyson (1904–1985)
Bud Hyson came to Gallup from Oklahoma to coach high school sports in the 1950s and 1960s and is still revered several generations later. Joe Vargas, one of his star basketball players, recalled, "Coach Hyson was one of those guys that said, 'I want to build gentlemen first, and the basketball player will come on his own.' He coached not for basketball but for life." (Courtesy of the *Gallup Independent.*)

Joe Yurcic (1913–1996)

In 1938, capping off a successful college career playing for New Mexico State in Las Cruces, Joe Yurcic was named both All Border Conference Tackle and the "Greatest Aggie." The only Gallup High School graduate with a professional football career, Yurcic played for both the New York Giants and the Pittsburgh Pirates. He also was a heavyweight boxer known as "One Punch Promo." Yurcic later opened a machine shop and ran a salvage yard while working for the local fire department. The World War II–era limousine once used by J. Robert Oppenheimer and other scientists from the Manhattan Project was retrieved from his salvage yard and taken to Albuquerque's National Museum of Nuclear Science and History for restoration and display. (Left, courtesy of Josephine Yurcic; below, photograph by Carol Sarath.)

Jerry Butler (1916–2000) and Grace Butler (1917–1992)

In 1951, the Pennsylvania couple Gerald "Jerry" and Grace Butler was looking to buy a printing and office supply business out West, either in El Paso or Gallup. The deciding factor? Neither spoke Spanish, so Gallup became the clear winner. Butler's first opened its doors at 203 West Coal Street, where Grace ran the retail store and Jerry ran the print shop. It is a division of labor their sons still follow. Barry runs the store, and Pat runs the printing business. The couple was active in civic affairs, another tradition their sons have emulated. According to Pat Butler, his parents lived by the principle that "we need to support the community that supported us." These portraits were done by Jacquelyn Kammerer Cattaneo. (Both, courtesy of the Butler family.)

Geronimo Martin (1917–1984) and Faye Edgerton (1889–1968)
Any Navajo speaker who picks up *Diyin God Bizaad*—the Navajo Bible—is holding a copy of a decades-long labor of love by numerous Navajo translators. Geronimo Martin, a blind Navajo Christian who dedicated his life to translating hymns and biblical scripture into the language of the Diné people, and Faye Edgerton, an Anglo missionary and Wycliffe Bible translator, were two of the most dedicated translators. The two, shown here with a Navajo elder in 1949, began working together in 1945, with Martin reading from a Braille King James Bible and translating into Navajo. Their work contributed to the publication of the Navajo New Testament in 1956. After Edgerton's death, Martin and his wife, Lois, continued to work on translating the entire Bible. Martin died in 1984, followed by the Navajo Bible's publication in 1986. (Photograph made available by Fuller Theological Seminary.)

Octavia Fellin (1918–2013)

"People should give of themselves to their community," said Gallup's beloved Octavia Fellin, and the legacy of excellence that followed her long tenure as director of the public library is evidence that Fellin lived her philosophy. In 1947, Fellin was just stopping by her hometown to spend a couple of months with her parents on her way to a job opportunity in San Francisco, when she met a challenge too great to pass up. It was Gallup's library—barely even in a state to be called a library—with books and magazines piled on tables, furniture in disrepair, and cracks in the wall that one could see through. And so Fellin converted a former jail with an outhouse into a functioning public library. She was so successful that a few years later she ran a campaign that resulted in a new library building, completed and opened to the public on December 22, 1951. Fellin went on to serve as the city librarian for more than 40 years. While winning awards for her library work, including the prestigious Dorothy Canfield Fisher Library Award and the New Mexico Library Association's Community Achievement Award and Honorary Lifetime Membership Award, Fellin was also active in many community organizations, including the local Chamber of Commerce, American Association of University Women, League of Women Voters, Plateau Sciences Society, and Gallup Inter-Tribal Indian Ceremonial Association. Fellin, a strong voice for women, was named one of the 30 Outstanding Women in New Mexico by Gov. Gary Carruthers in 1988. As one of 10 women named to the US Catholic Bishops' National Advisory Council, she supported a broader role for women in the church, going so far as to advocate in favor of women priests. A proponent of social justice causes, Fellin was also a strong supporter of the Catholic sisters involved in the Nuns on the Bus tours. Fellin traveled widely and met Helen Keller, Eleanor Roosevelt, Mother Teresa, and Pope John XXIII. When she retired in 1990, the library was renamed in Fellin's honor. Under the direction of current librarian Mary Ellen Pellington, and building on the service and standards established by Fellin, the Octavia Fellin Public Library was awarded the National Medal of Museum and Library Service in 2014. The award was presented by First Lady Michelle Obama in a ceremony at the White House. (Courtesy of Octavia Fellin Public Library.)

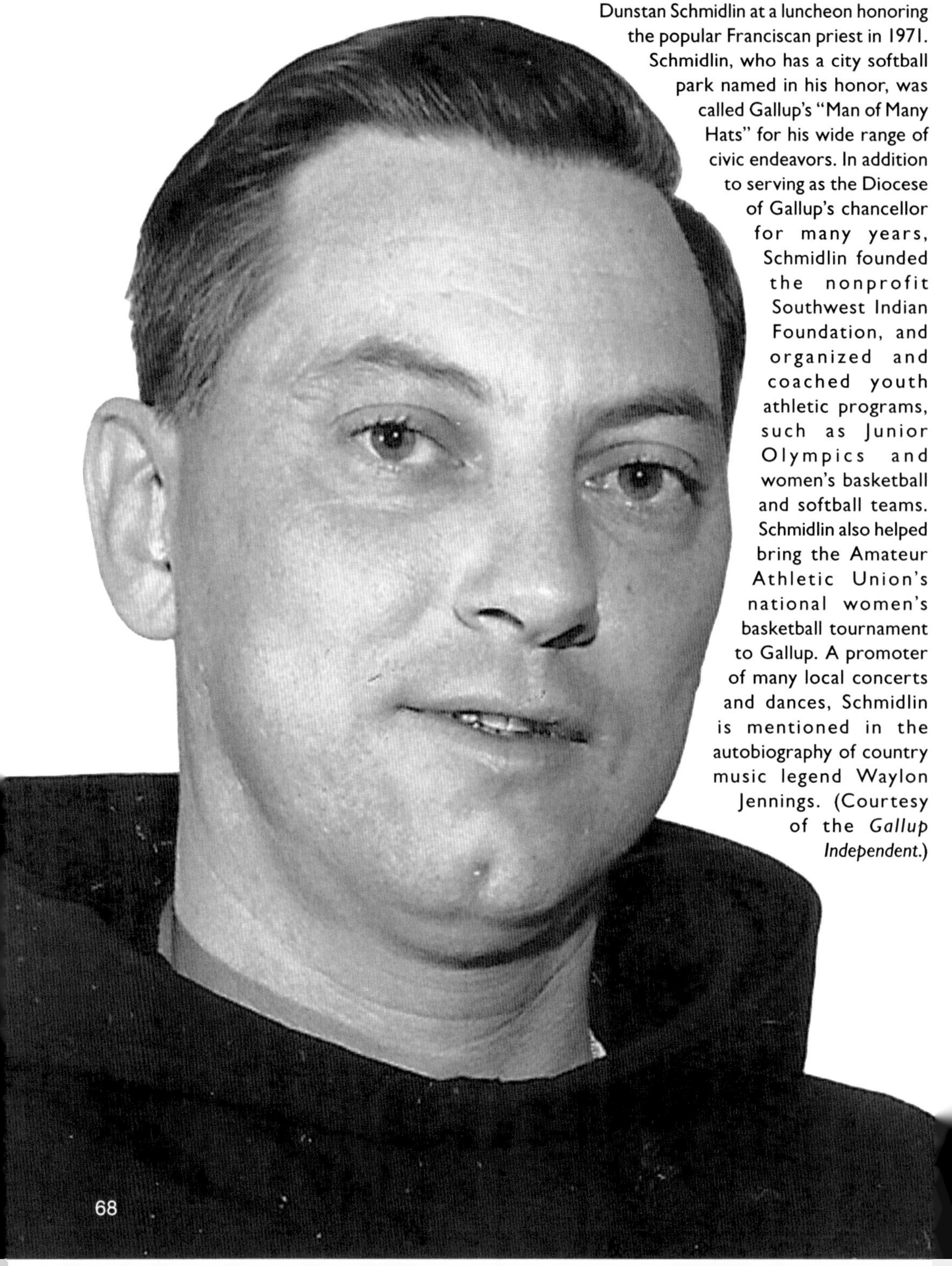

Father Dunstan Schmidlin (1921–1989)

"No politician could draw a crowd like this, even when the meals are free," Gallup mayor Ray Erwin said of Father Dunstan Schmidlin at a luncheon honoring the popular Franciscan priest in 1971. Schmidlin, who has a city softball park named in his honor, was called Gallup's "Man of Many Hats" for his wide range of civic endeavors. In addition to serving as the Diocese of Gallup's chancellor for many years, Schmidlin founded the nonprofit Southwest Indian Foundation, and organized and coached youth athletic programs, such as Junior Olympics and women's basketball and softball teams. Schmidlin also helped bring the Amateur Athletic Union's national women's basketball tournament to Gallup. A promoter of many local concerts and dances, Schmidlin is mentioned in the autobiography of country music legend Waylon Jennings. (Courtesy of the *Gallup Independent*.)

Father Cormac Antram (1926–2013)
Dubbed "the Holy Wind Talker" by a *Los Angeles Times* writer, Father Cormac Antram spent nearly 60 years as a Franciscan friar in Gallup and the Navajo Nation. Fluent in Navajo, Antram became well-known among the Diné people through his long-running, popular weekly Navajo radio program, *The Padre's Hour.* (Courtesy of the Archives of the Franciscan Province of Our Lady of Guadalupe of Albuquerque.)

Virgie Mazon Chavez (1921–1996)
Virgie Mazon Chavez grew up in the historic ranching community of Atarque. Chavez opened her first restaurant in 1968 and was always the driving force behind her family business. Although the restaurant moved to several locations, Virgie's customers always followed, seeking their favorite Mexican food specialties. Virgie's Restaurant, now operated by her son Charlie Chavez, still uses the same recipes today. Pictured are Virgie and Timoteo Chavez. (Courtesy of Charlie Chavez.)

John K. Zollinger (1921–2007)

Had it not been for two crucial life decisions by John K. Zollinger, the late owner and publisher of the *Gallup Independent* newspaper, Gallup and Navajo tribal government would be much different today. The first was Zollinger's decision to go into the newspaper business and not the ministry. The second was to purchase the *Independent*, rather than other newspapers he was looking at elsewhere in the country. A native of Ohio, Zollinger had been a first lieutenant in the Army Air Corps during World War II, serving as a navigator in the Pacific theater. After the war, Zollinger worked as a newspaper advertising salesman, sales manager, and publisher. By 1963, however, he was looking to own his own newspaper. On January 1, 1964—a month before the Beatles' historic performance on *The Ed Sullivan Show*—Zollinger purchased the *Independent* from Lincoln O'Brien of Farmington. With the sale, the *Independent* became a locally owned newspaper for the first time since 1952 and Zollinger began to transform the struggling small-town paper into a multicultural regional newspaper. He devoted energy into expanding the paper's news coverage, its territory, and its circulation. Within a decade, Zollinger had created a Diné Bureau to cover Navajo tribal government, and the *Independent* became the first off-reservation newspaper in the Four Corners to include in-depth Navajo and Native American news in its daily coverage. And with the *Independent*'s growing readership among Native Americans, its advertising brought families from neighboring Navajo and Pueblo communities to shop in Gallup and boost the city's role as a shopping mecca for the region. In addition, Zollinger continually invested money to keep the newspaper's technology and equipment up to date—to get the news into the hands of readers more quickly and efficiently. Zollinger also became a generous civic leader in Gallup, known particularly for his support of UNM-Gallup, as well as Rehoboth McKinley Christian Hospital. Zollinger and his wife, Martha, suffered a devastating loss in 1968 when their 15-year-old daughter Mary Ann died from heart failure after running in P.E. class. The couple helped establish the Zollinger Library and an academic scholarship at UNM-Gallup in Mary Ann's memory. In 2004, the Navajo Nation honored Zollinger with the rarely bestowed Friend of the Navajo Award. (Courtesy of the *Gallup Independent*.)

Martha Zollinger (1922–) Known for her sunny smile, quick humor, funny "Martha-isms," and for cruising town in her red Mustang, Martha Zollinger has one of the community's most upbeat, forever-young personalities. Named 2011 Volunteer of the Year by the Gallup Chamber of Commerce, Zollinger jokes she has been a "street walker" for hustling charity raffle tickets, a "bag lady" for bagging food at the Community Pantry, and a "bookie" for her contributions to Zollinger Library at UNM-Gallup. Zollinger credits her joyful public service to the emotional turnaround she experienced after struggling with the death of her daughter in 1968. While assisting friends with missionary work in Panama, Zollinger realized helping others takes the focus off one's own problems. "I like to make people smile," she says. "If they don't have one, I give them one of mine." (Courtesy of Perry Null Trading Company.)

Niram Alan Wilson Jr. (1927–2000)
Alan Wilson could be considered the father of the Red Rock Balloon Rally. He and his wife, Kaye, were two of the first local hot-air balloonists, and he taught a ballooning class that inspired the balloon rally founders. Although born and raised in Gallup, Wilson was a scholar, teacher, author, linguist, athlete, poet, musician, and artist who traveled the world. He joined the Marines, attended the University of Southern California on a football scholarship, transferred to Harvard University and graduated Summa Cum Laude, and later worked for the US intelligence service as a Russian interpreter. Through the years, Wilson taught French, Spanish, German, Serbo-Croatian, Russian, and Navajo. He also studied Arabic, Indonesian, Yiddish, and Hebrew as well. Wilson authored 12 books, with six focused on the Navajo language. (Both, courtesy of the *Gallup Independent.*)

Sally Noe (1926–2015)
Sally Noe made Gallup's history, people, and culture her life's work. A history teacher at Gallup High and UNM-Gallup, Noe published three books and 35 articles about Gallup. In addition, she collected oral histories of Gallup's old families, which are now available online through UNM Special Collections. Noe never met a stranger when she had a chance to talk about the history and allure of Gallup. (Courtesy of Kathe Noe.)

Mildred Holmes (1929–2012)
Passing through Gallup on a train trip, Mildred Holmes fell in love with the town and vowed to return. Later, with an adventurous spirit, Holmes and her husband made good on her promise when they moved to Prewitt to begin long teaching careers here. After retirement, Holmes volunteered with the National Association for the Advancement of Colored People (NAACP), First Baptist Church, and the Gallup Inter-Tribal Indian Ceremonial. Four local academic scholarships honor Holmes's legacy as an influential educator. (Courtesy of the *Gallup Independent*, Brian Leddy.)

Sister Gloria Davis (1933–2000)

Just weeks after graduating from Cathedral High School in 1952, former homecoming queen Gloria Davis left Gallup to travel to Pennsylvania to become the first local Native American woman to join the Sisters of the Blessed Sacrament. Davis, who was Navajo and Mississippi Choctaw, served nearly 50 years as a Catholic sister in the order founded by St. Katharine Drexel. After attending Drexel's canonization ceremony in Rome October 1, 2000, Davis told one of her sisters, "Oh, I'm so happy, I don't mind if

God takes me tomorrow." Two weeks later, Davis died in Fort Defiance, Arizona. Davis is shown at the Second Annual Prayer Pilgrimage for Peace, Chimayo to Los Alamos, New Mexico, in April 1984. (Courtesy of the Archives of the Sisters of the Blessed Sacrament.)

Martin Link (1934–)
Martin Link's first visit to Gallup mirrored the experience of thousands of other Americans traveling on historic Route 66. The visit occurred when he was 12 years old, traveling with his family on their way to their new home in California. They stayed in Gallup's landmark El Rancho Hotel and liked it so much that they returned each year on their summer trips back to their native Wisconsin. Link could not have known then what this community would hold in store for him, nor could he imagine he would someday build a home and a professional career here. After graduating from the University of Arizona with majors in anthropology and history, Link returned to the Gallup region, where he has lived for almost 60 years. He has devoted his life to the study of the archaeology and history of the Southwest. Link's lengthy career includes being a ranger-archaeologist at Canyon de Chelley National Monument, an archaeologist for the Navajo Tribe conducting field work in conjunction with the Navajo-Hopi land dispute, director of the Navajo Nation Tribal Museum in Window Rock and manager of Red Rock State Park in Gallup, publisher of the *Indian Trader* newspaper, instructor at the University of New Mexico-Gallup, and author of several books, including *Navajo: A Century of Progress* and the ever popular children's book *The Goat in the Rug*. Link's most recent book, *New Mexico Kicks on Route 66,* was published in 2016, coinciding with the 90th anniversary of the establishment of Route 66. Link was chairman of the Gallup Centennial Committee, which celebrated the city's 100th year in 1981, and designed Gallup's first official flag for the occasion. Link is active in the Plateau Sciences Society and a number of other civic organizations. An avid collector of Southwestern art, Link offers workshops for collectors on important artists and their work. Link is shown standing next to a piece in his art collection, Navajo artist Irving Toddy's painting that depicts the signing of the Treaty of 1868 between the Diné people and the federal government. (Photograph by Carol Sarath.)

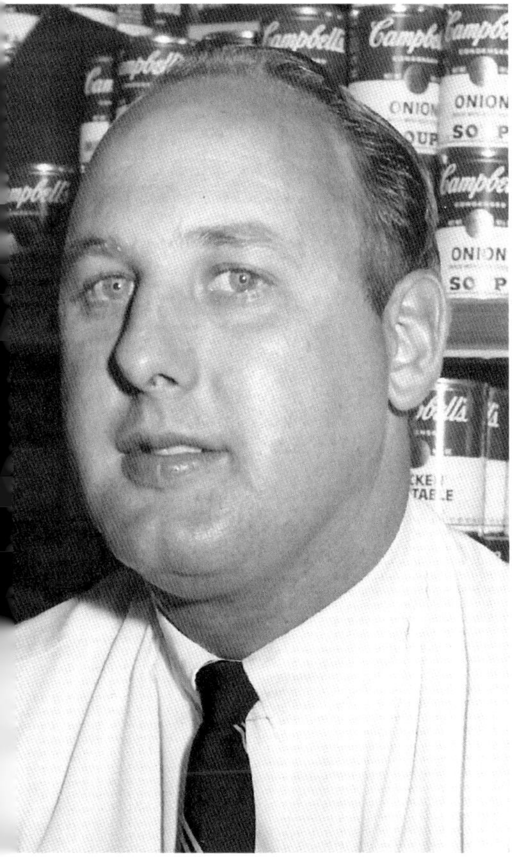

Paul McCollum (1936–)

Paul McCollum is Gallup's longest-tenured city manager, having served with five mayors. McCollum grew up in a time when anything seemed possible in Gallup's business community. He remembers when a builder came to develop Sunset, Linda Vista, and Valley View Drives. The builder was struggling until he went to a civic luncheon. "They sold 24 houses there at a Rotary meeting at noon," McCollum recalled. "That's what got that development started up there on Mortgage Hill." (Courtesy of the *Gallup Independent.*)

Sherwood and Roberta Stauder (Both 1938–)

Roberta Stauder's grandfather John Novak emigrated from Austria and worked first in the coal mines as a carpenter and later as a builder. In 1939, Novak learned a downtown lumberyard was going up for sale. That was the beginning of Gallup Lumber. At Sherwood Stauder's initiative, the business moved to its current location, where after four generations of family management, it continues to serve the building needs of the local community. (Courtesy of the Sheree Stauder.)

Sharon D. Richards (1934–2017) and Ralph Richards (1953–)

In 1979, Sharon Richards, a waitress at Earl's, purchased the restaurant from its original owner. A year later, her son Ralph Richards (pictured) returned to Gallup and began working his way up the ranks of the popular eatery. Earl's, known for its homemade favorites and Native American vendor program, has been featured in travel magazines, documentaries, and national television programs. (Courtesy of the *Gallup Independent*, Brian Leddy.)

Johnny Espinosa (1934–)

Johnny Espinosa was a catcher for the 1953 Gallup High state championship baseball team. After a brief stint in California, Espinosa returned to Gallup to coach youth baseball for 40 years. Espinosa recalled, "I always told the kids that I coached: 'Baseball is life. It's your life. You have to compete for something whether it's your girlfriend, whether it's a job, whatever it is.' " (Courtesy of Chuck Van Drunen.)

Mary Jean Christensen (1938–)
Gallup businesswoman Mary Jean Christensen, of Elite Laundry, is a civic-minded dynamo and Gallup booster. Christensen has been active in state agencies and organizations such as the New Mexico Highway Commission and New Mexico First, and local organizations such as the Gallup-McKinley County Chamber of Commerce Legislative Gallup Days Committee, Adventure Gallup, the Downtown Business Improvement District, and the Gallup Inter-Tribal Indian Ceremonial. (Courtesy of the *Gallup Independent*, Cable Hoover.)

Frank Kozeliski (1944–)
At just seven years old, Frank Kozeliski started working at Gallup Sand and Gravel. Through the years, Kozeliski developed a statewide reputation for his skills. A contractor who specialized in building public schools once said, "Mixing concrete is both a science and an art. Frank was a master of both." In 2007, 61 years after Gallup Sand opened, Kozeliski retired and his family sold the business. (Courtesy of Chuck Van Drunen.)

Jim Harlin (1944–2011)

When Jim Harlin moved to Gallup in 1997 from Yuma, Arizona, he immediately immersed himself in the community. His overarching goal was to help feed the most vulnerable people in the community—the elderly and the young. Harlin's motto was, "No mother's child should go hungry." After his death in 2011, the Community Pantry, which he founded, was named after him. (Courtesy of the *Gallup Independent*, Jeff Jones.)

Joe Vargas (1938–)

After returning from the Korean War, Joe Vargas went to work for the city. When he became director of parks and recreation in 1962—a position Vargas held for almost four decades—there were only three parks in Gallup: Ford Canyon, Viro, and Bubany Park. By the end of his career, Gallup had 23 parks, and his greatest satisfaction was restoring the once neglected veterans cemetery. (Courtesy of Chuck Van Drunen.)

Emma Estrada (1933–1997)
The first childbirth Emma Estrada ever assisted was that of her own baby sister. When icy streets prevented the doctor's arrival, 10-year-old Estrada ran four blocks to fetch a *partera*, or midwife. Estrada grew up to be a well-known Gallup midwife, and became the first Hispanic midwife in New Mexico to be medically licensed by the state. Gallup's historical marker by the *We the People* sculpture honors Estrada. (Courtesy of Raymond Estrada.)

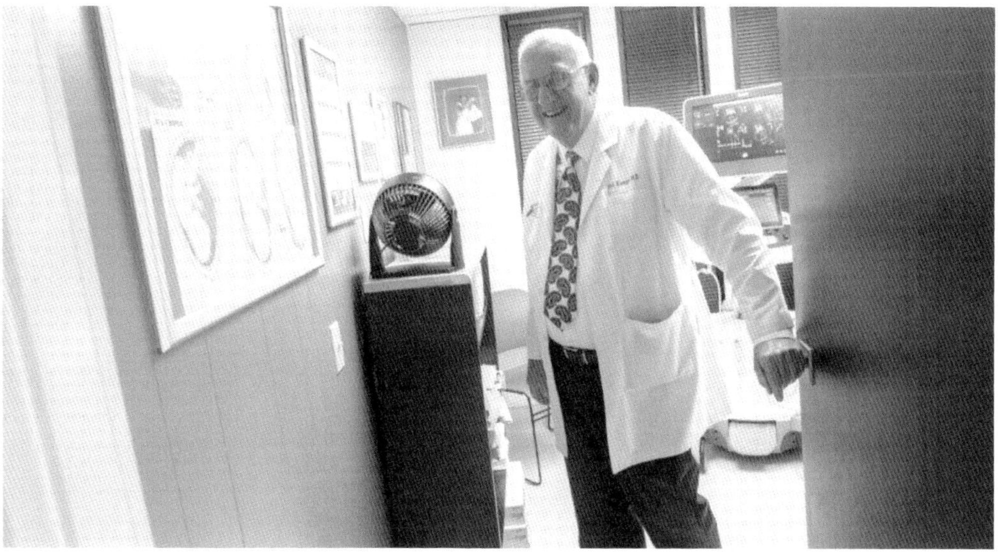

Phil Kamps (1939–)
The longest practicing obstetrician and gynecologist in Gallup, Dr. Phil Kamps estimates he has delivered "somewhere over 7,000" babies in his career—or about one-third of the population of Gallup. Although he averaged about four or five deliveries a week, there were occasional baby booms of up to 25 babies in the space of a few days. Kamps himself never would have been born here if not for events in China in the 1920s. His parents, Jacob and Isabel Kamps, were Christian Reformed missionaries who planned to work in China, but political unrest blocked that path. Instead, they agreed to serve as missionaries in Rehoboth for just one year. They ended up staying permanently and raising six sons in Rehoboth. Phil Kamps, now semiretired, continues to provide ultrasounds for expectant mothers. (Courtesy of the *Gallup Independent*, Adron Gardner.)

Bill Donovan (1946–)

In 1970, Bill Donovan was a cub reporter working the crime beat in his native Kentucky when a Navajo law enforcement officer—working in Kentucky—suggested Donovan move west and cover the Navajo Nation. The officer, with tongue firmly in cheek, also told Donovan he would need to learn Native American sign language. Donovan took the advice to heart and secured a job with the *Farmington Daily Times*. He also bought Iron Eyes Cody's sign language book, which he diligently studied on the road trip. Once in New Mexico, Donovan's *Farmington* job evaporated, but he was hired by the *Gallup Independent* as a sports reporter. Donovan soon became the paper's first Diné Bureau reporter. More than 45 years later, Donovan is still covering the people and politicians of Gallup and the Navajo Nation. (Above, courtesy of E. Hardin-Burrola; left, courtesy of Bill Donovan.)

John McBreen (1946–)
After graduating from the University of Oklahoma with a degree in mass communication and journalism, John McBreen found himself looking for work. On one memorable day, he went from interviewing Pres. Lyndon Johnson back to his regular job as a dishwasher. But McBreen proved talented at landing interviews and landing professional work. After answering an ad in *Broadcasting Magazine* in 1973, McBreen has spent the rest of his career as the lone radio newsman in Gallup, covering local news of the city, county, and reservation. McBreen has interviewed every governor since he arrived in New Mexico. His 12 Mark Twain Awards for broadcasters and numerous AP awards and citations reflect his journalistic excellence, but the fact that local radio in Gallup still supports his show indicates McBreen's popularity with his listeners. (Photograph by Bill Siebersma.)

Dr. Bruce Tempest (1931–)

On May 14, 1993, Dr. Bruce Tempest, a commissioned officer with the US Public Health Service and director of medicine at the Gallup Indian Medical Center (GIMC), was confronted with a medical mystery. It was a mystery that would soon grab national headlines. A 19-year-old Navajo man who was having trouble breathing showed up in the GIMC emergency room. Within an hour, the man, who had been athletic and otherwise healthy, was dead. His fiancée had died days before—also from breathing problems. Something was different and troubling about these cases. Tempest began working systematically to review other cases and catalogue symptoms. He contacted other doctors in the area, along with the medical examiner, and sought help from the New Mexico Health Department. Soon, the Center for Disease Control joined the effort. News media accounts, which for a time called the illness the "Four Corners Disease," were causing widespread alarm, and tourists began avoiding Gallup and the Navajo Nation. Young, previously healthy individuals were dying rapidly after acquiring this mystery illness. After a massive effort by dozens of doctors and epidemiologists, the disease was identified several weeks later as Hantavirus Pulmonary Syndrome (HPS), a severe cardiopulmonary disease previously experienced by American and Korean soldiers in the early 1950s, although in a less deadly form and with a somewhat different disease pattern. The 1993 outbreak was the first time the disease had been identified in the western hemisphere. Although hantavirus, which is spread by deer mice urine and droppings, has been identified, there is still no known cure. The disease is transmitted to humans by inhalation of the deer mice urine and droppings or direct rodent contact. Rodent control remains the primary prevention strategy. New Mexico remains the state with the highest number of cases, and more than one third of hantavirus patients die. (Courtesy of Chuck Van Drunen.)

Ron Polinder (1946–) and Colleen Polinder (1946–2012)
Longtime educators Ron Polinder and his late wife, Colleen, helped usher Rehoboth Christian School into the 21st century. Under Ron Polinder's leadership from 2000 to 2009, the school built a new middle school, sports center, and science lab and replaced its aging campus infrastructure. Polinder believes the school also managed to build better relationships with the Native American and Gallup communities. (Courtesy of the *Gallup Independent*, Cable Hoover.)

Carol Bremer-Bennett (1969–)
Carol Bremer-Bennett became the first Native American and first woman to lead Rehoboth Christian School when she became school superintendent in 2010. She broke those same barriers in 2015, when she moved to Michigan to become US director of World Renew, the international charity of the Christian Reformed Church. Bremer-Bennett, far left, and her husband, Theo, far right, are shown here with their six children in 2015. (Courtesy of Rehoboth Christian School.)

Angelo DiPaolo (1948–2014) and Phil Garcia (1948–2015)

Lifelong friends Angelo DiPaolo and Phil Garcia met in Cathedral Grade School. Although they took different career paths, their civic and professional contributions built Gallup into a better community. DiPaolo established a respected reputation as a teacher, coach, administrator, and athletic director during a 39-year career that included positions at the Window Rock School District, the Gallup-McKinley County Schools, and Gallup Catholic School. He was posthumously inducted into the New Mexico Activities Association's Hall of Fame in 2015. Garcia, the owner of Gallup Title Company, served on the Gallup Planning and Zoning Commission for nearly 40 years and on numerous civic boards. A former school board president and county assessor, Garcia contributed to the beautification of downtown Gallup with the addition of his new office building, designed to complement the adjacent historic courthouse. (Both, courtesy of the *Gallup Independent*, Jeff Jones and Adron Gardner.)

Karl Lohmann (1948–)
In 1973, new teacher Karl Lohmann arrived in town after the Gallup schools offered him more money than any other district. And so, for the grand annual salary of $7,300, Lohmann began to teach elementary school and coach basketball, a sport he had never played. In the years since, Lohmann has been a prime mover in a multitude of programs and organizations: a children's summer bookmobile program, the Red Rock Balloon Rally, Playground of Dreams, Trek for Trash, Tree Amigos, a kids' bike mobile project, VISTA volunteers, Boys and Girls Club, Youth Conservation Corps, Adventure Gallup, and Work in Beauty. A common thread running through all these endeavors has been the goal of improving the quality of life in Gallup, particularly for children. "No investment in youth is ever wasted," Lohmann says. (Courtesy of Carol Sarath.)

Armand Ortega (1928–2014)

The first time Armand Ortega saw Gallup's El Rancho Hotel he was 13 years old and was captivated by its grandeur. When Ortega died at the age of 86, he was called its savior for restoring it to its former glory. In his later years, Ortega was as well recognized as the landmark hotel itself—regularly drinking coffee or buying jewelry at the Gallup hotel that he saved from ruin. (Courtesy of the *Gallup Independent.*)

Curtis Williams (1949–)

In 1982, during his fourth year as coach of Gallup High's cross country team, Curtis Williams came to a pivotal moment. His team should have qualified for the state championships at the IAAAA meet, but they fell short. Williams boarded the team bus and asked a question. "Guys, what did we do wrong?" One of the kids replied, "Coach, you didn't work us hard enough." When Williams got back to his office he wrote, "Work the hell out of them," on a three-by-five card and stuck in on his bulletin board. Beginning in 1983, Gallup won 12 consecutive boys' team titles, and later won two more state titles before Williams retired in 2003. The girls' program started slower, but also became a juggernaut—winning 11 team titles during his tenure. His runners won 17 individual state championships. (Courtesy of Curtis Williams.)

John Lomasney (1948–2011)
For 28 years, Lomasney prowled the courtside in front of huge, passionate Gallup High basketball crowds while his girls' teams frustrated opponents with a patient, disciplined offense and a harassing man-to-man defense. An opposing coach once said, "He played a style that drove you crazy and forced you to adapt." Throughout his reign, Lomasney wore garish black and orange attire with wide suspenders, and his thunderous voice could be heard over the loudest crowds. By the end, Lomasney had won 503 games to 187 losses and reached the state championship game six times. His teams brought back the championship trophy to Gallup four times: 1994, 1997, 2002, and 2006. Named Coach of the Year three times, Lomasney was inducted into the New Mexico High School Coaches Hall of Honor in 2006. (Courtesy of the *Gallup Independent*, Jeff Jones.)

Mother Magda Garcia (1939–)
Since Mother Magda Garcia and her Sisters of Our Lady of Guadalupe and St. Joseph founded their ministry and Casa Reina Chapel of Perpetual Adoration in Gallup in 1976, Garcia has become one of the Catholic community's most beloved and respected figures. Mother Magda Garcia is known for her compassion for the poor, advocacy for immigrants, devotion to prayer, and Christ-like kindness to all. (Courtesy of the *Gallup Independent*, Jeff Jones.)

Jay McCollum (1953–)
A native of Port Arthur, Texas, Jay McCollum became pastor of First Baptist Church in 1994. Since then, he has helped local students receive college scholarships through the Rotary Club and has been the driving force behind the local World Changers program. With his booming voice and Texas accent, at first blush, McCollum seems out of place in Gallup, but he has the strength of character—the "grit in the gizzard," as he would say—to be a true community builder. (Courtesy of Jay McCollum.)

Grant L. Foutz (1947–)
In 1996, a bipartisan judicial nominating committee met and considered several applicants to serve as a district judge. The committee decided that only one applicant, Grant L. Foutz, a Democrat, was qualified. Foutz's name was sent to the Republican governor, who declined to make the appointment. The governor requested additional names from which to choose. The committee reconvened and again found that Foutz was the only qualified applicant. When the governor refused a second time to make the appointment, the New Mexico Supreme Court broke the political standoff and appointed Foutz to the bench. After that controversial start, Foutz presided on the district court bench for 18 years with a calm demeanor, wry sense of humor, and well-grounded knowledge of the law. He now serves as Gallup's municipal court judge. (Courtesy of the *Gallup Independent*, Adron Gardner.)

Joyce Graves (1949–) and Linda Shelton (1948–)

Receiving a cancer diagnosis when one is facing a classroom of kindergarten students is a tough challenge. Local teacher Joyce Graves (below, with her mother, Elizabeth Higgins) took it in stride and went on to establish a hugely successful Relay for Life in Gallup, which has raised more than a million dollars. Fellow teacher Linda Shelton (left) came on board after her mom's diagnosis and then her own. Graves has attended and presented at regional and national trainings and has been a cancer research advocate in Washington, DC. Shelton is the creator of the most popular Relay for Life fundraising event, the annual birdhouse auction. This duo works tirelessly to support local people experiencing cancer, from diagnosis through treatment. (Both, courtesy of John Van't Land.)

Bill Siebersma (1950–)

Bill Siebersma's family moved to Fort Wingate in the late 1960s, and he has been in love with the Zuni Mountains ever since. Siebersma is one of the principal mountain bike trail designers in the Zunis, which are known nationally for their sweeping, natural flow. Siebersma's goal is to design trails that cause cyclists to become absorbed into the experience. (Courtesy of the *Gallup Independent*, Brian Leddy.)

Alex McAllister (1947–)

When Alex McAllister was named the new head football coach at Gallup High in 1977, the school had not had a winning season for over a decade. Within two years, Gallup was no longer a AAAA doormat. During his tenure, McAllister's teams won seven district 1AAAA championships. In 1999, McAllister was selected to the New Mexico High School Coaches Hall of Honor. (Courtesy of *Gallup Journey*.)

Mona Frazier (1951–)

Originally from New Orleans, Mona Frazier is widely known for her community service. In addition to organizing Gallup's annual Martin Luther King Jr. Day celebration for many years, Frazier has volunteered with Connections, the NAACP, Boys and Girls Club, Crime Stoppers, and St. Paul's Missionary Baptist Church. Now retired from Safeway, Frazier was named a Safeway Community Hero in 2004. (Courtesy of the *Gallup Independent*, Cable Hoover.)

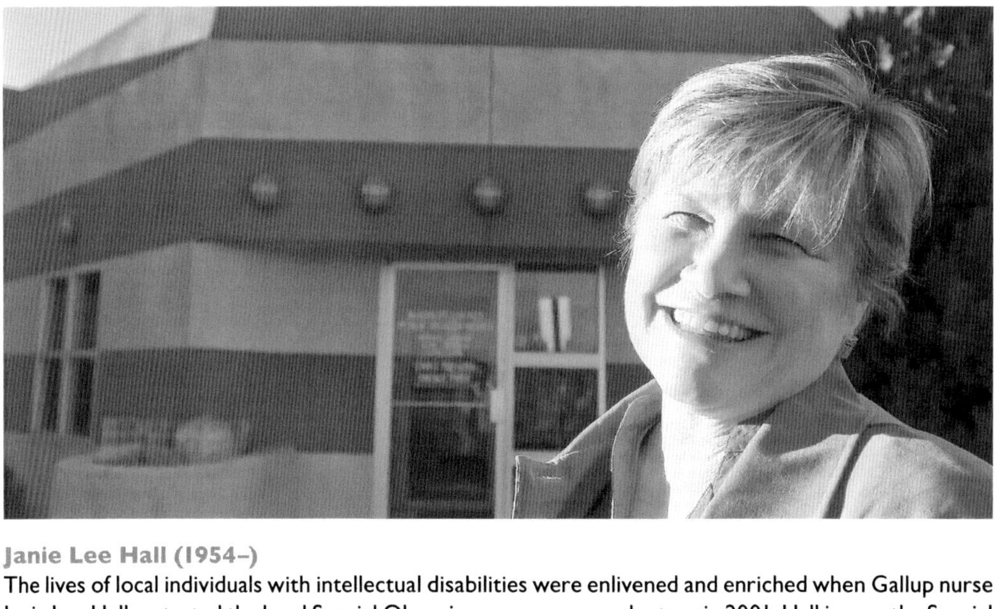

Janie Lee Hall (1954–)

The lives of local individuals with intellectual disabilities were enlivened and enriched when Gallup nurse Janie Lee Hall restarted the local Special Olympics program as a volunteer in 2001. Hall is now the Special Olympics New Mexico Area 6 director and plans and coordinates the area's year-round competition in track and field, bocce, volleyball, aquatics, golf, softball, basketball, and bowling for McKinley and Cibola Counties. (Courtesy of the *Gallup Independent*, Matt Hinshaw.)

Red Rock Balloon Rally Founders

So how did a lost ferret lead to the founding of Gallup's Red Rock Balloon Rally? In 1980, hot-air balloonists found a lost ferret wandering the streets. The ferret happened to belong to Mary Jean Christensen, a member of the chamber of commerce, and one thing led to another. Christensen invited the balloonists to present their idea of a Gallup balloon rally to the chamber. Peter Procopio, Karl Lohmann, and Lionel McKinney made their successful pitch, and the result was the first Red Rock Balloon Rally in December 1981. The idea was to promote the use of Red Rock Park as a balloonist destination, not only to showcase its spectacular ballooning characteristics, but also to bring tourist dollars to the city during a month when no other large events were scheduled. While the first year drew 30 balloonists, the popular event has grown to include as many as 200. The rally is now a major asset for the Gallup community. The Red Rock Balloon Rally has an international reputation built over the years by many founders. They have worked tirelessly to create an event that includes a flying venue that cannot be matched, community participation, and business support. Favorite rally activities include the evening balloon glows and balloonists' participation in Gallup's annual Christmas Parade. Procopio, who has remained active with the Red Rock Balloon Rally Association, has said, "Many balloonists and spectators have commented that watching hundreds of colored balloons glide in and out of the red rock canyons is one of the most beautiful sights they have ever seen." Bill Lee, current president of the chamber, has been with the Red Rock Balloon Rally almost as long as the founders. He is a fixture at pilot briefings and has become the face of the rally. Lee also flies region-wide and has been known to fly such dignitaries as Gov. Susana Martinez and student winners of summer reading contests. Lee's newest balloon is named *True-Lee New Mexico.* (Both, courtesy of the *Gallup Independent*, Brian Leddy and Jeff Jones.)

Salvatore "Sammy C" Chioda (1954–)

Born and raised in Gallup, Salvatore "Sammy C" Chioda seems to have radio in his blood. At age 14, he began working at the same radio station where he is now company president and still an on-air personality. A self-taught broadcaster, Chioda learned sports announcing by listening to regional and national sports programs. He went on to initiate a successful broadcast for the statewide high school cross country meet. Chioda has also been the voice of Gallup's Inter-Tribal Indian Ceremonial since 1980, one of only four in the organization's history. Chioda was inducted into the New Mexico Broadcasters Hall of Fame in 2005. In addition, he established Sammy C's Rock N' Sports Pub and Grille, which was named one of CNN's 101 Best Sport Bars in the United States. (Courtesy of the *Gallup Independent*, Cable Hoover.)

Dudley Byerley (1954–)
As a young man, Dudley Byerley won the bareback and bull riding events in Ramah on both Saturday and Sunday. Since then, rodeo has remained a constant in his life. During one five year stretch, Byerley put on 36 rodeos a year. He was directly responsible for bringing the National Junior High Rodeo to Gallup for a nine-year run that ended in 2014. (Courtesy of the *Gallup Independent*, Adron Gardner.)

Walt Eddy (1957–)
In high school, Walt Eddy was a state champion in the team roping event at the New Mexico High Schools Finals Rodeo. In the 1980s, Eddy returned to the sport as a promoter and developed Gallup's Red Rock Classic as well as putting on United States Team Roping Championships events in Moab, Las Cruces, Albuquerque, and Scottsdale. At its height, the Red Rock Classic drew 3,500 teams from 17 states. (Courtesy of the *Gallup Independent*, Cable Hoover.)

Patty Lundstrom (1959–)
Patty Lundstrom was first elected to the New Mexico House of Representatives in 2001 and continues serving today as the longest-tenured representative in Gallup's history. Once Lundstrom takes on a task, whether it is the Navajo Gallup Water Supply Project, promoting adventure tourism for Gallup, or regulating predatory lending practices, she has a history of finishing what she starts. (Courtesy of the *Gallup Independent*, Brian Leddy.)

Cosy Balok
After a childhood rescuing animals on Coronado Island, California, Cosy Balok has made rescuing animals her lifework as director of the Gallup–McKinley County Humane Society. Once a high-kill shelter, the organization now boasts a low-kill shelter, strong education program, low-cost spay and neuter clinics, and a program that annually sends 5,000 dogs to other cities for adoption. Balok is pictured with her veterinarian husband, Clint. (Courtesy of Cosy Balok.)

Mary Ann Armijo (1958–)
A native of Northern New Mexico, Mary Ann Armijo became interested in politics on a junior high field trip to Santa Fe's Legislative Round House. After moving to Gallup—and a short stint as a Republican—Armijo's political career began modestly as Parent Teacher Organization president. She then became active as chair of McKinley County's Democratic Party, which she has continued for 30 years. Armijo also served a term as a Gallup city councilor. Rising to challenges in her life and career, Armijo has always pushed herself to succeed. She is now general manager of the radio station where she began working in sales almost three decades ago. During Gov. Bill Richardson's tenure, Armijo was named chair of the state's Commission on the Status of Women, and she attended Pres. Barak Obama's inauguration. (Courtesy of the *Gallup Independent*, Brian Leddy.)

Rick Murphy (1962–)
After earning an engineering degree, Rick Murphy returned to Gallup and has become the contractor of choice for large projects. His company has built Gallup's Aquatic Center and six schools in McKinley County, completed three major school remodels, and built or remodeled almost every bank in town. His favorite jobs have been Indian trading businesses "because of the uniqueness of the customers and their creativity." (Courtesy of Chuck Van Drunen.)

Betty Armstrong (1949–)
Betty Armstrong has worked in real estate for over 40 years and owned the Gallup Century 21 franchise for 30 of those years. Throughout her career, Armstrong has been a steady, calming voice helping people in Gallup find their way through life-changing events. Gallup's Nightly Indian Dances were initiated while she was president of the chamber of commerce. (Courtesy of Chuck Van Drunen.)

Sandra Begay-Campbell (1963–)

Sandra Begay-Campbell says she grew up with leadership in her blood. She is the daughter of the late Cecila M. Begay, an Indian Health Service nurse, and Edward T. Begay, the former vice-chairman of the Navajo Nation and first speaker of the Navajo Nation Council. Begay-Campbell has fond childhood memories of spending time at the rural Church Rock Chapter House and is proud to be called a Gallupian. Begay-Campbell, a graduate of Rehoboth High School and the University of New Mexico, has a master's degree in structural engineering from Stanford University. Her current job with Sandia National Labs is to provide technical assistance to American Indian and Alaska Natives in strategic energy planning. Begay-Campbell is the recipient of numerous honors, including the American Indian Science and Engineering Society's Lifetime Achievement Award. (Courtesy of Randy Montoya, Sandia National Laboratories.)

Loren Miller (1962–)
Loren Miller is one of the few individuals to be successful in both the Gallup and Navajo Nation business worlds. His company, LAM Corporation, offers design and construction services for both residential and commercial projects. Miller's favorite project was the Rehoboth Christian School's Sports and Fitness Center. He was involved in the 2007 project from inception through completion. (Courtesy of the *Gallup Independent*, Adron Gardner.)

Peter Tempest (1964–)
In 1999, Peter Tempest wrote *The Gallup Guide: Outdoor Routes in Red Rock Country.* The guide describes local mountain biking, road biking, hiking, cross country skiing, and rock climbing routes. After Tempest's book came out, new hiking and mountain biking trails have been developed on private, city, state, Bureau of Land Management, and US Forest Service land. The city also purchased a rock climbing area and developed a bike park near downtown. (Courtesy of Peter Tempest.)

Felicia Guliford (1984–)
Beginning in eighth grade, Felicia Guliford ran track and cross country for Gallup High, winning 24 state championships. She still holds unbroken state records. Guliford received a full scholarship to the University of Tennessee, where she was Student Athlete of the Year and graduated Magna Cum Laude. She is pictured with her father, Lawrence, a longtime basketball, track, and cross country coach. (Courtesy of the *Gallup Independent*, Jeff Jones.)

Onawa Lacy (1982–)
Gallup High graduate Onawa Lacy became the first woman to represent Gallup in either a Miss America or Miss USA pageant when she won the Miss New Mexico USA 2006 title. Lacy, who is Navajo and Anglo, was previously Miss Indian New Mexico 2001–2002 and Miss Indian World 2003–2004. Now a practicing attorney, Lacy is pictured with her grandmother Ella Mae Yazzie. (Courtesy of the *Gallup Independent*, Julie Peña.)

Sanjay Choudhrie (1961–)

In 2004, Sanjay Choudhrie moved to Gallup and helped found CARE 66 Inc. He has since devoted his professional life to addressing homelessness in Gallup. It is a mission with roots in family history. When Choudhrie's great-grandfather died in India under mysterious circumstances, women could not inherit property, so Choudhrie's great-grandmother was suddenly left destitute. To survive, she began working at a boarding school run by Swedish missionaries. When asked about his path in life, Choudhrie says, "I don't know if I'm paying back the kindnesses that were shown to my great-grandmother or investing in the future of my kids." Under Choudhrie's guidance, CARE 66 serves 500 to 1,000 people a year. The organization has also built 30 housing units at Chuska Apartments, 44 units at Hooghan Hozho, and remodeled the Lexington Hotel. (Courtesy of the *Gallup Independent*, Adron Gardner.)

CHAPTER FOUR

Creative Voices

The Gallup region has been home to people who have been making their mark—literally and artistically—on the landscape for millennia. From the petroglyphs of the ancient Anasazi, to the signatures of the Spanish explorers at El Morro, to the boldly painted murals in contemporary downtown Gallup, people have been creating art, dancing, writing, making music, and telling stories for generations.

These generations of creative voices have combined to create Gallup's multicultural mix of artistic expression. The following pages tell just a few of the stories of the many artists and entertainers, dancers and designers, muralists and musicians, painters and photographers, and storytellers and writers. They have shared their artistic visions and pushed the boundaries of what art is. In their lives and work, they have caused people to consider new ideas and perspectives.

While Gallup is rightly proud that some of the finest Native American jewelry is imagined, created, and marketed here, the diversity of talented artists and artisans in this community is unlimited. The city is filled with public art, created by artists from all walks of life. The city's downtown mural project, created to celebrate local history and culture, has inspired more murals across the community. Gallup's monthly ArtsCrawl has grown from an evening of small art exhibits to a large and lively community celebration. Between Gallup's popular indoor and outdoor venues—El Morro Theatre, Coal Avenue, and the courthouse square—local audiences can enjoy a variety of music and entertainment that ranges from country to classical, gospel to hip hop, opera to rock, Spanish music to Native dances, and more. The Octavia Fellin Public Library also regularly gets in on the action by offering public presentations by storytellers, writers, and performers.

Artistic tradition is big in Gallup, but so is artistic innovation. Like some of the area's culinary favorites—Navajo tacos, Mexican pizza, and green chile apple pie—the local artistic community is always mixing up artistic traditions to create something amazing.

Ben Wittick (1845–1903)
Ben Wittick was one of the preeminent photographers who documented the people and landscapes of the Southwest. Hired by the Atlantic & Pacific Railroad in 1878 to document western expansion, Wittick later opened a number of photography studios, including one in downtown Gallup and his final studio at Fort Wingate. Wittick traveled with an assortment of costumes, painted backgrounds, and props to stage many of his portraits, including his own self-portrait, at left. One of his most famous photographs was of Chiricahua Apache leader Geronimo (below). Wittick died in 1903 after catching a rattlesnake near Fort Wingate that he intended to give to Hopis during a visit to their villages. His death by snakebite had reportedly been foretold by a Hopi snake priest. (Left, courtesy of the Palace of the Governors Photo Archives, NMHM/DCA, No. 074477; below, courtesy of the National Archives, photograph No. 111-SC-83726.)

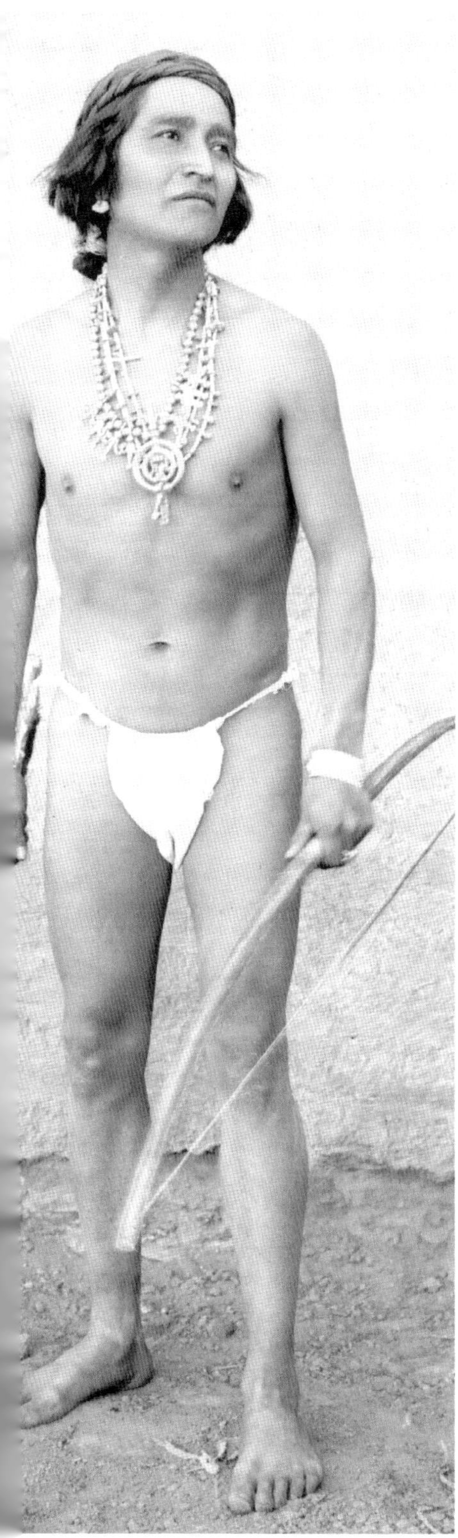

Simeon Schwemberger (1867–1931)

A Native of Cincinnati, Ohio, Brother Simeon Schwemberger came to the Southwest in 1901 as a Franciscan friar assigned to the Catholic mission in St. Michaels, Arizona. Not particularly interested in the daily drudgery of mission life, Schwemberger discovered his talent for photography when he began experimenting with photographic equipment purchased by the mission for archival purposes. From 1902 to 1908, Schwemberger captured more than 1,700 images in travels across the Navajo Reservation and visits to the Hopi, Cochiti, Jemez, and Zuni Pueblos. Using a large-format camera that recorded images on coated glass plates, Schwemberger documented life at Indian missions, captured sweeping Southwestern landscapes, and photographed the daily activities and ceremonies of Native American people at the turn of the 20th century. In 1908, Schwemberger, who was not suited for a life as a Franciscan friar, left St. Michaels to pursue an ill-fated romance in Gallup, taking the mission's photography equipment and glass-plate negatives. When the romance did not work out, Schwemberger established his Indian Arts Studio in Gallup, where he marketed his photographs and postcards and sold Native American crafts. Over the next decade, Schwemberger married and moved between Gallup and the Navajo Reservation, working as a merchant, postmaster, and Indian trader. In 1923, Schwemberger married his second wife, Margaret Sandy, and the couple's daughter, Eunice, would go on to eventually marry into Gallup's noted Fellin family. Before Schwemberger's death, his family returned the photography equipment and extensive glass-plate negative collection to the Franciscan Friars at St. Michaels. The friars eventually placed the negative collection with Arizona State University, which has cataloged and performed high-resolution scans of each image. The Simeon Schwemberger Franciscan Southwest Mission Photographs have since been written about in numerous news stories and scholarly articles and featured in gallery exhibits. Schwemberger's pioneering photography is also the subject of Paul V. Long and Michele M. Penhall's book *Big Eyes: The Southwestern Photographs of Simeon Schwemberger, 1902–1908*, published by the University of New Mexico Press. This c. 1909 photograph by Schwemberger is titled "Zuni Marathon Racer—Figure Study." In a *Gallup Journey* article, local author Ernie Bulow identified this runner as Old Man Laate from Zuni Pueblo. (Courtesy of the Library of Congress, item No. 90711308.)

Roger M. Zimmerman (1936–)
With the publication of his book *Kitchen's Opera House*, Roger M. Zimmerman transitioned from a career as a civil engineer to a new role as Gallup storyteller. Born at the old Rehoboth Mission Hospital, Zimmerman grew up next to the opera house when his father began operating Zimmerman's Dry Goods Store. Zimmerman is pictured inside Gallup's historic Eagle Café in 2012. (Courtesy of the *Gallup Independent*, Adron Gardner.)

Carl Boller (1868–1946)
Noted theater designer Carl Boller, of the architectural firm Boller Bros. from Kansas City, built Gallup's El Morro Theatre as a "castle of pleasure and art" in 1928. Boller Bros. also built the Kimo Theatre in Albuquerque and the Lensic Theatre in Santa Fe. El Morro Theatre is the only example of Spanish Colonial Revival architecture in Gallup. (Courtesy of Gallup Historical Society.)

Carl N. Gorman (1907–1998)

The citation on Carl Gorman's doctor of humane letters from the University of New Mexico in 1990 reads, "Painter, teacher, philosopher, soldier, healer." Gorman was truly a Renaissance man whose life and talents impacted the history and culture of the Navajo Nation, Gallup, and the greater society. Growing up at the remote, but beautiful, mouth of Canyon de Chelly, Gorman was nurtured by his remarkable mother, Alice. She insisted that he be allowed to have the time to develop his artistic gift, and exposed him to the unlikely art form of opera, which proved to be one of Gorman's lifelong loves. Alice had traded one of her beautifully woven rugs for a phonograph and a stack of records. They listened repeatedly to the recordings while Carl drew pictures of horses—despite his father's wishes that he do more work around the home. Gorman's art career was put on hold during World War II when he was recruited as one of the original 29 Navajo Code Talkers by the US Marine Corps. After the war, Gorman studied art at the Otis Art Institute in Los Angeles, and later taught Native American art and helped develop the Native American Studies program at the University of California, Davis. The C.N. Gorman Museum at UC Davis, to which he contributed not only his name but some of his artifacts, is dedicated to promoting Native American art. Gorman became recognized as an innovative and distinguished painter, and his award-winning artwork was displayed in many national and international museums. He and his wife, Mary, moved back to the region in 1973, where he began working on projects to benefit Navajo artists and veterans, including directing the Navajo Arts & Crafts Guild, founding the Navajo Code Talkers Association, and working on a project that collected oral histories of Navajo elders. In addition, Gorman also spent time teaching at both the Navajo Community College and UNM-Gallup. Gorman was the father of R.C. Gorman, an artist who gained international fame, and Zonnie Gorman, who has worked with her father to promote and preserve the history of the Navajo Code Talkers. One of Gorman's good friends in Gallup, fellow artist Jacqueline Cattaneo, remembers Gorman as an "accomplished teacher, lecturer, activist, leader, and connoisseur of fine art and culture." (Courtesy of the C.N. Gorman Museum, University of California, Davis.)

Dr. Alex Seowtewa (1933–2014)

Alex Seowtewa, a member of the Zuni Pueblo, lost his mother when he was just three years old. His father and maternal grandfather, both historians and religious leaders, provided him with a foundation in both the traditional Zuni religion and the Catholic faith. Seowtewa was studying art at the College of St. Joseph in Albuquerque until his studies were interrupted by the Korean War. Upon his return, Seowtewa worked at St. Anthony's Mission in Zuni, where he provided for his wife, Odelle, and his growing family of 10 children. In 1966, excavation and renovation efforts began on Zuni's old mission church, Nuestra Senora de Guadalupe, or Our Lady of Guadalupe, with Gallup contractor and stone mason Auro Cattaneo heading up the restoration work. Seowtewa was asked by Father Niles Kraft, a Franciscan friar working in Zuni, if he would be interested in crafting a confessional for the renovation. Seowtewa's father had told him stories of the paintings that had once decorated the old mission church depicting Zuni Kachinas, or deities, as fierce ogres and disciplinarians. Seowtewa proposed he be allowed to paint a new series of murals on the walls of the renovated church that would meld similarities between Catholicism and Zuni spirituality and would document and preserve Zuni history. The project began in 1970, and would eventually take 25 years to complete and include the work of Seowtewa and three of his sons. Seowtewa became the recipient of numerous awards and honors for his lifework at the Zuni mission church. In 1991, he received the award for Excellence in Art from New Mexico governor Bruce King. Seowtewa also received the New Mexico Preservation Heritage Award from the New Mexico Cultural Affairs office. In 2006, he was named an Arizona Indian Living Treasure. Seowtewa traveled around the world to discuss his work, and the world has traveled to the Pueblo of Zuni to view the church murals of the "Michelangelo of Zuni." Celebrated visitors have included former First Lady Jacqueline Kennedy Onassis and Mother Teresa. Seowtewa is shown in these photographs perched on scaffolding, working on his mural at Our Lady of Guadalupe Mission Church. (Courtesy of the Seowtewa family.)

Tony Hillerman (1925–2008)
Best-selling and award-winning author Tony Hillerman famously ignored an early editor's advice to "get rid of that Indian stuff" and went on to write 18 Joe Leaphorn/Jim Chee Navajo mysteries, beginning with *The Blessing Way* in 1970 and ending with *The Shape Shifter* in 2006. Hillerman was born in Sacred Heart, Oklahoma, and grew up attending school with students from the Potawatomie Tribe. He attributed his interest in and respect for Native American people and culture to his early school experiences. A longtime journalist, Hillerman later taught journalism at the University of New Mexico. As an author, Hillerman wrote 30 books and received many literary awards. But perhaps his most cherished award was from the Navajo Nation. According to local reporter Bill Donovan, former Navajo chairman Peter MacDonald was a Hillerman fan. At MacDonald's prompting, the Navajo Nation Council passed a resolution naming Hillerman a Friend of the Navajo Nation. Hillerman also received an informal Navajo nickname, which he said translated as, "He who is afraid of his horse." Through the years, Hillerman came to know Gallup, and some of its residents, very well. Hillerman coauthored *Talking Mysteries* with Ernie Bulow, wrote a foreword for Larry Linford's *Tony Hillerman's Navajoland,* and made Gallup attorney Bob Rosebrough a character, by his real name, in *The Fallen Man*. Hillerman enjoyed including real people as fictional characters in his novels. In the opening scene of *The Fallen Man,* Hillerman describes a lithe rock climber perfectly traversing a vertical rock wall using only the tips of his toes and his fingertips—humorously giving the climber the name of one of Hillerman's heavyset poker playing buddies. Hillerman appreciated the awards and good reviews he received, but he once said, "I am far more delighted by being voted the most popular author by students of St. Catherine Indian School, and even more by middle-aged Navajos who tell me that reading my mysteries revived their children's interest in the Navajo Way." (Courtesy of Anne Hillerman.)

Be Sargent (1940–)

For a muralist, a blank wall is a canvas beckoning to be painted. And for Be Sargent, there was more than one blank wall in Gallup that needed to be painted, and more than one story that needed to be told. In 2001, Sargent got her chance to paint the *Navajo Code Talker* mural, one of eight downtown murals she oversaw for the City of Gallup's mural project. Each mural is unique in style and content, depicting stories of historical events, local places, and cultures. For the *Navajo Code Talker* mural, Sargent consulted with code talker Albert Smith, who emphasized the importance of the Navajo language. Sargent is also a founder of Work in Beauty, a nonprofit whose mission is to increase local agriculture through education, demonstration gardens, and workshops. (Courtesy of the *Gallup Independent*; inset, courtesy of Milan Sklenar.)

Bob Dylan (1941–)

So why did rock legend Bob Dylan, who grew up as Robert Zimmerman, the son of an appliance dealer in Hibbing, Minnesota, spin fanciful tales to journalists about growing up or living in Gallup as a kid? There are a lot of different theories, but here is the one proposed by the *Gallup Journey* in September 2010: "That at some point as a youngster Dylan was driving with his family through Gallup on Route 66. Well, what did he see as he drove through town? A huge sign smack dab in the middle of a town filled with Indians and cowboys that said 'Zimmerman's.' And when it came time to invent a persona to match the image of 'the freewheelin' Bob Dylan' he thought back to that sign and the town where he saw it." This poster image was created by Gallup artist Ric Sarracino for the gallupArts Bob Dylan Tribute Concert in June 2017. (Courtesy Ric Sarracino.)

Ernie Bulow (1943–)
On his first trip to Gallup in 1960, writer Ernie Bulow and his two traveling companions were stopped in traffic, taken to jail, and interrogated all night by police. According to Bulow, "A couple of little girls had been shot at a ranch just across the line in Arizona and they were looking for suspicious guys, and boy did we fit the bill." When their alibis checked out, Bulow and his friends were released. Bulow came back six years later when his wife took a teaching job at Fort Wingate, and he suddenly found himself teaching several classes when the school was short of teachers. On weekends, Bulow immersed himself in the culture of his Navajo students. Those weekend trips and his students' stories were the inspiration for the first of Bulow's six books, *Navajo Taboos*. (Courtesy of Chuck Van Drunen.)

Tom Funk (1948–)
Volunteering at his college radio station started Tom Funk on his lifelong interest in music. After moving to Gallup, Funk followed the founding of public radio station KGLP, which finally went on air in 1992. Funk joined the station as a board member and then as a local program producer. Now KGLP's music director, he hosts Saturday afternoon's popular *Green Chile Revival and Medicine Show.* (Courtesy of Carol Sarath.)

Milan Sklenar (1941–)
Born in Czechoslovakia under a Soviet system that did not foster his pursuit of film studies, Sklenar attended film school and got a degree in art history in Canada. After stints in New York City and Los Angeles, Sklenar settled in Gallup, where he taught photography and art history at UNM-Gallup. In 1985, he opened Crashing Thunder Studio, which hosted art exhibits and quickly became a local gathering place. (Courtesy of Milan Sklenar.)

Jacquelyn Kammerer Cattaneo (1944–)

Jacquelyn Kammerer Cattaneo was a 15-year-old student in Winona Pulley's Gallup High School art class when she realized she was meant to be an artist. "There was something that awakened some vibes in me that said you've got to do this," Cattaneo recalled. In the years since, Cattaneo has become one of Gallup's most successful artists, known for her portraits and landscapes. According to Cattaneo, three of her favorite portrait subjects have been strong women: Mother Katharine Drexel, Mother Teresa, and Octavia Fellin. She painted the first two women—now canonized as saints—for Gallup's Sacred Heart Cathedral. She portrayed Fellin, her close friend, in Fellin's role as Gallup's longtime, beloved librarian. Cattaneo has also enjoyed teaching youth art classes because it gives children the opportunity to express themselves. (Courtesy of the *Gallup Independent*, Brian Leddy.)

Carolyn Milligan (1943–)

From her first visit to Gallup's public library, artist Carolyn Milligan (right) was hooked. The library's collection of paintings by Works Progress Administration artists and her many conversations with librarian Octavia Fellin left Milligan fascinated by WPA art and architecture in Gallup. Milligan has since spent years researching the Roosevelt administration's New Deal initiative that put artists and craftsmen to work in the 1930s. With Gallup and McKinley County home to a large and impressive WPA art collection, Milligan has worked with special emphasis to document the WPA art in the McKinley County Courthouse. She also helped oversee the restoration of Herman NcNeil's historic statue of Manuelito. WPA artist Lloyd Moylan is pictured above painting the McKinley County Courthouse mural. Carolyn Milligan is pictured in front of the restored Chief Manuelito statue. (Above, courtesy of Octavia Fellin Public Library, Nello T. Guadagnoli; right, photograph by Carol Sarath.)

Kenji Kawano (1949–)

Photographer Kenji Kawano, a native of Fukuoka, Japan, first arrived in Gallup on a Trailways bus in 1974. He had come to photograph the Western landscape and get to know the Navajo people, promising his parents he would only stay in the United States for three months. It was a promise he would not keep. Kawano's ideas about Native Americans and the American West—formed by watching Western movies with his father—were soon upended by the real people he met. One such meeting proved to be life changing. In the summer of 1975, Kawano was hitchhiking when he was picked up by artist Carl Gorman, one of the original 29 Navajo Code Talkers, along with Gorman's wife, Mary. Kawano was astounded to hear the story of the code talkers and learn how the Diné language had been used as a weapon against the Japanese military. That chance encounter marked the beginning of Kawano's long relationship with the Navajo Code Talkers, and in one of life's ironies, the Japanese photographer was eventually named an honorary Navajo Code Talker and the official photographer for the group. During his life here, Kawano met and married his wife, Ruth, a member of the Navajo Nation, and published several books, including *Warriors: Navajo Code Talkers*, and a book with aerial photographer Adriel Heisey, *In the Fifth World: Portrait of the Navajo Nation*. Kawano has shown his work in numerous galleries in the United States and Japan. His exhibit *40 Years with the Navajo* was featured at the Navajo Nation Museum in 2015. As a photographer, the Navajo people and their dramatic landscape continue to capture Kawano's imagination. Indeed, photographing them has become his lifework. A memorable experience was when Kawano was able to take his father to Monument Valley, one of the places they had both seen in movies, and a place that had inspired him to visit Navajo land in his youth. A promise Kawano has kept was one he made to his wife—to always portray the people he photographs with dignity and respect. This is evident in Kawano's impressive body of work. (Courtesy of Baznibah Photography.)

Bill Krzymowski (1954–)
A physician at the Gallup Indian Medical Center and a classically trained musician, Bill Krzymowski helped established the Red Rock String Ensemble in 2004. The ensemble now features more than 20 local musicians and attracts professional guest musicians for its popular concerts. Krzymowski, who plays the violin and viola, also regularly performs internationally with the nonprofit World Civic Orchestra and World Doctors Orchestra. (Courtesy of the *Gallup Independent*, Brian Leddy.)

Richard "Dick" Chavez (1943–)
When he was 10 years old, Dick Chavez saw two elderly blind musicians—a husband and wife—playing accordions downtown during the Gallup Ceremonial. Mesmerized by the duo, Chavez soaked in their music. He soon bought an accordion and learned to play. When he was 33, Chavez began playing publicly. Since then, he has played a wide variety of musical genres with more than a dozen groups. (Courtesy of the *Gallup Independent*, Brian Leddy.)

Ric Sarracino (1958–)

Ric Sarracino describes drawing in the kitchen—on paper bags or any scrap paper he could find—while his family watched scary television movies. Although Sarracino learned construction from his dad, he says he was an artist trapped in a contractor's body. Sarracino has painted many of the most important murals in Gallup, including the *Community Life* mural on Gallup City Hall. (Photograph by Carol Sarath.)

Gallup Journey Founders

In 2004, Chuck Van Drunen, a believer in the power of positive press, convinced his wife, Jenny, and his friends Nate and Heather Haveman and Chuck Whitney to quit their jobs and take a leap of faith to create the *Gallup Journey*. The popular free monthly magazine—with the slogan "believe Gallup"—has gone from being delivered on bicycles to being distributed across the community. Pictured are Nate Haveman (left) and Chuck Van Drunen. (Courtesy of Nate Haveman.)

Bob Ippel (1959–) and Gail DeYoung (1954–)

One of Gallup's most beautiful Christmas traditions is the annual Christmas concert by the Rehoboth Christian High School Choir at Sacred Heart Cathedral, under the direction of choir directors Bob Ippel and Gail DeYoung. Ippel, originally from Michigan, is a former teacher and now Rehoboth Middle School principal. Iowa native DeYoung is a Rehoboth counselor and teacher. The pair, who teamed up to establish the choir in the mid-1990s, has since gone on to direct award-winning choirs, train a number of students who are now professional musicians, and release a series of choir CDs. DeYoung believes music classes like choir and band touch the hearts of students and gives them a personal voice and strength in a way academic classes cannot. (Above, courtesy of the *Gallup Independent*, Nicole Goodhue; left, courtesy of John Van't Land.)

Virginia Yazzie Ballenger (1957–)

Award-winning fashion designer Virginia Yazzie Ballenger first showed an interest in fashion at age five, when she designed clothing for her paper doll that was inspired by the fashions in her sister's Montgomery Ward catalog. Later, as a young woman, Yazzie Ballenger learned to sew on her mother's old treadle sewing machine to create outfits for the pageants she was entering. Her sewing and design skills blossomed as she won numerous titles, beginning with Gallup High School Princess 1974–1975, to later titles as Miss Indian Ceremonial 1980 and Miss Indian New Mexico 1982. Eventually, her hobby of sewing clothing for herself grew into her successful Navajo Spirit Southwestern Wear company in Gallup, and her fashion design career has taken her to countries such as Russia and South Africa. (Courtesy of Virginia Yazzie Ballenger.)

Adriel Heisey (1957–)

Growing up on a farm in Carlisle, Pennsylvania, Adriel Heisey's first thought of getting airborne was when he watched the moon landing on television and decided he wanted to become an astronaut. Inspired by reading *Flying* magazine in his junior high library, Heisey built a full-size hang glider at the age of 14. He saved up for private flying lessons and soloed at the age of 16. While in college, Heisey decided he wanted to make flying his career, and became a successful pilot on the East Coast. However, a yearlong experience in Kinlichee, Arizona, exposed him to the spectacular beauty of the Navajo Nation. Of that time, Heisey has recalled, "The arid landscape of earth and sky seemed mythic and monumental." When faced with another career path decision, Heisey made the choice to return to the reservation. That brought him to his 30-year career as a pilot for the Navajo Nation, where he has flown a variety of tribal leaders. During this time, Heisey has been able to combine his love of flying with what he found to be his calling, the art of aerial photography. Heisey built a small plane that allowed him to fly low and slow over the Southwestern terrain so he could pilot and photograph at the same time. He has since become an acclaimed aerial photographer whose work has been featured in magazines, books, and art exhibitions. Heisey collaborated with photographer Kenji Kawano for their book *In the Fifth World: Portrait of the Navajo Nation*, and published two books of his aerial photographs: *Under the Sun: A Sonoran Desert Odyssey*, and *From Above: Images of a Storied Land*. In addition, Heisey photographed the Rio Grande River along its entire length for a book titled *The Rio Grande: An Eagle's View*. In recent years, Heisey retraced Charles and Anne Lindbergh's 1929 route through the Southwest, recreating their photographs, some of the earliest aerial images taken of major landmarks and archaeological sites such as Canyon de Chelly and Chaco Canyon. Heisey's photographs, along with the early Lindbergh images, were paired for the exhibit *Oblique Views: Archaeology, Photography, and Time* at Santa Fe's Museum of Indian Arts and Culture in 2015. (Copyright Adriel Heisey.)

Sunny Dooley

Diné storyteller Sunny Dooley is from Chichiltah, south of Gallup. When she won the Miss Navajo title in 1982, Dooley was the first contestant to use storytelling for her traditional talent. She has gone on to share *Hane'*—Diné Origin, Creation, and Blessing Way stories—with the world in schools, colleges, conferences, and theaters, throughout North America, Africa, and Europe. (Photograph by Lisa Rodriguez, courtesy of Sunny Dooley.)

Victor Bob (1958–)

Noted powwow dancer Victor Bob started dancing at age 10 in his mother, Lorine's, Indian Club in Seba Dalkai, Arizona, when powwows were not common in the Navajo Nation. He traveled with his father, Jimmy, a singer with a drum group, and competed with his brother Rudy across the Southwest. Bob assists with Gallup's New Year's Eve Sobriety Powwow and Relay for Life. (Courtesy of Marty Thompson Photography.)

James Junes (1970–) and Ernie Tsosie III (1967–)

James and Ernie, the Navajo Nation's Kings of Comedy, teamed up after competing in a Native comedy contest. Masters of improv, the duo bounce off each other with high-octane energy as they spoof contemporary life. Tsosie (left), a Gallup High graduate, and Junes are also both actors and frequently focus on societal struggles through the lens of comedy and laughter. (Courtesy of James and Ernie.)

Greg Ballenger (1996–)

Local artist Greg Ballenger has literally made his mark on Gallup. In 2014, while still in his teens, Ballenger painted his first mural of a veteran—his uncle Eugene Attcity—on a wall downtown. The success of that first mural led Ballenger to paint a series of striking mural portraits of veterans. In 2015, Ballenger created a large portrait of Manuelito for Chief Manuelito Mid-School. (Courtesy of the *Gallup Independent*, Adron Gardner.)

INDEX

LEGENDARY
LOCALS

AN IMPRINT OF ARCADIA PUBLISHING

Find more books like this at
www.legendarylocals.com

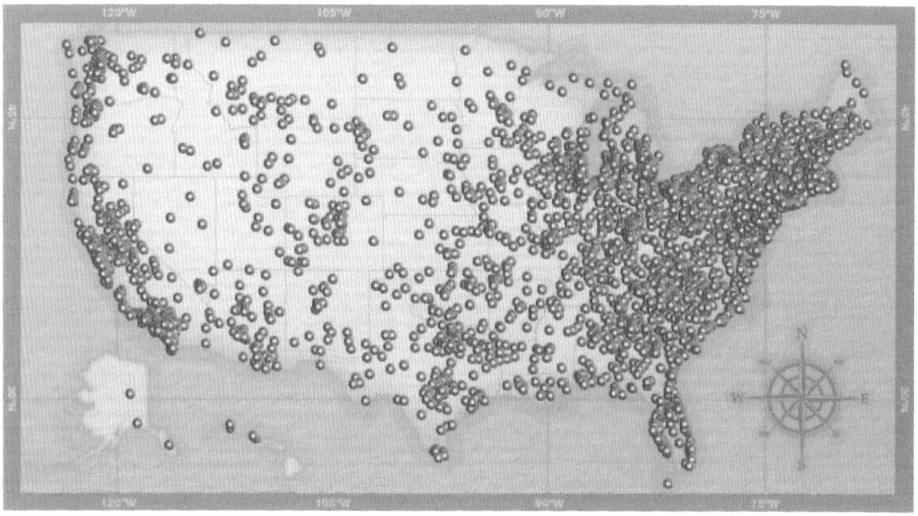

Discover more local and regional history books at
www.arcadiapublishing.com

Consistent with our mission to preserve history on a local level, this book was printed in South Carolina on American-made paper and manufactured entirely in the United States. Products carrying the accredited Forest Stewardship Council (FSC) label are printed on 100 percent FSC-certified paper.

MADE IN THE USA